AT YOUR
COMMAND

AT YOUR COMMAND

Deluxe Edition

Neville Goddard

*Includes a Biographical Essay and Timeline
by PEN Award-Winning Historian*

Mitch Horowitz

MEDIA

MEDIA

Published 2022 by Gildan Media LLC
aka G&D Media
www.GandDmedia.com

Front cover design by David Rheinhardt of Pyrographx

Library of Congress Cataloging-in-Publication Data is available upon request

ISBN: 978-1-7225-0588-2

10   9   8   7   6   5   4   3   2   1

CONTENTS

I

AT YOUR COMMAND

LETTER FROM NEVILLE

*This book contains the very essence
of the Principle of Expression. Had
I cared to, I could have expanded it
into a book of several hundred pages
but such expansion would have
defeated the purpose of this book.*

*Commands, to be effective, must be short
and to the point: the greatest command
ever recored is found in the few simple
words, "And God said, 'Let there be light.'"*

*In keeping with this principle I now give
to you, the reader, in these few pages,
the truth as it was revealed to me.*

—NEVILLE

INTRODUCTION

You do not command things to appear by your words or loud affirmations. Such vain repetition is more often than not confirmation of the opposite. Decreeing is ever done in consciousness. That is; every man is conscious of being that which he has decreed himself to be. The dumb man without using words is conscious of being dumb. Therefore he is decreeing himself to be dumb.

Instead of looking upon the Bible as the historical record of an ancient civilization or the biography of the unusual life of Jesus, see it as a great psychological drama taking place in the consciousness of man. Claim it as your own and you will suddenly transform your world from the barren deserts of Egypt to the promised land of Canaan. Every one will agree with the statement that all things were made by God, and without him there is nothing made that is made, but what man does not agree upon is the identity of God. All the churches and priesthoods of the world disagree as to the identity and true nature of God. The Bible proves beyond the shadow of a doubt that Moses and the prophets were in one hundred per cent accord as to the identity and nature of God. And Jesus' life and teachings are in agreement with the findings of the prophets of old. Moses discovered God to be man's awareness of being, when he declared these little understood words, "I AM hath sent me unto you." David sang in his psalms, "Be still and know that I AM God." Isaiah declared, "I AM the Lord and there is none else. There is no God beside me. I girded thee, though thou hast not known me. I form the light, and create darkness; I make peace, and create evil. I the Lord do all these things."

The *awareness of being* as God is stated hundreds of times in the New Testament. To name but a few: "I AM the shepherd, I AM the door; I AM the resurrection and the life; I AM the way; I AM the Alpha and Omega; I AM the beginning and the end"; and again, "Whom do you say that I AM?"

Every one will agree with the statement that all things were made by God, and without him there is nothing made that is made, but what man does not agree upon is the identity of God. All the churches and priesthoods of the world disagree as to the identity and true nature of God. The Bible proves beyond the shadow of a doubt that Moses and the prophets were in one hundred per cent accord as to the identity and nature of God. And Jesus' life and teachings are in agreement with the findings of the prophets of old. Moses discovered God to be man's awareness of being, when he declared these little understood words, "I AM hath sent me unto you." David sang in his psalms, "Be still and know that I AM God." Isaiah declared, "I AM the Lord and there is none else. There is no God beside me. I girded thee, though thou hast not known me. I form the light, and create darkness; I make peace, and create evil. I the Lord do all these things."

The *awareness of being* as God is stated hundreds of times in the New Testament. To name but a few: "I AM the shepherd, I AM the door; I AM the resurrection and the life; I AM the way; I AM the Alpha and Omega; I AM the beginning and the end"; and again, "Whom do you say that I AM?"

AT YOUR COMMAND

Can man decree a thing and have it come to pass? Most decidedly he can! Man has always decreed that which has appeared in his world and is today decreeing that which is appearing in his world and shall continue to do so as long as man is conscious of being man. Not one thing has ever appeared in man's world but what man decreed that it should. This you may deny, but try as you will you cannot disprove it, for this decreeing is based upon a changeless principle. You do not command things to appear by your words or loud affirmations. Such vain repetition is more often than not confirmation of the opposite. Decreeing is ever done in consciousness. That is; every man is conscious of being that which he has decreed himself to be. The dumb man without using words is conscious of being dumb. Therefore he is decreeing himself to be dumb. So he is dumb.

When the Bible is read in this light you will find it to be the greatest scientific book ever written. Instead of looking upon the Bible as the historical record of an ancient civilization or the biography of the unusual life of Jesus, see it as a great psychological drama taking place in the consciousness of man.

Claim it as your own and you will suddenly transform your world from the barren deserts of Egypt to the promised land of Canaan.

Every one will agree with the statement that all things were made by God, and without him there is nothing made that is made, but what man does not agree upon is the identity of God. All the churches and priesthoods of the world disagree as to the identity and true nature of God. The Bible proves beyond the shadow of a doubt that Moses and the prophets were in one hundred per cent accord as to the identity and nature of God. And Jesus' life and teachings are in agreement with the findings of the prophets of old. Moses discovered God to be man's awareness of being, when he declared these little understood words, "I AM hath sent me unto you." David sang in his psalms, "Be still and know that I AM God." Isaiah declared, "I AM the Lord and there is none else. There is no God beside me. I girded thee, though thou hast not known me. I form the light, and create darkness; I make peace, and create evil. I the Lord do all these things."

The *awareness of being* as God is stated hundreds of times in the New Testament. To name but a few: "I AM the shepherd, I AM the door; I AM the resurrection and the life; I AM the way; I AM the Alpha and Omega; I AM the beginning and the end"; and again, "Whom do you say that I AM?"

It is not stated, "I, Jesus, am the door. I, Jesus, am the way," nor is it said, "Whom do you say that I, Jesus, am?" It is clearly stated, "I AM the way." The awareness of being is the door through which the manifestations of life pass into the world of form.

Consciousness is the resurrecting **power**—resurrecting that which man is conscious of being. Man is ever out-picturing that which he is conscious of being. This is the truth that makes man free, for man is always self-imprisoned or self-freed.

If you, the reader, will give up all of your former beliefs in a God apart from yourself, and claim God as your awareness of being—as Jesus and the prophets did—you will transform your world with the realization that, "I and my father are one." This statement, "I and my father are one, but my father is greater than I," seems very confusing—but if interpreted in the light of what we have just said concerning the identity of God, you will find it very revealing.

Consciousness, being God, is as "father." The thing that you are conscious of being is the "son" bearing witness of his "father." It is like the conceiver and its conceptions. The conceiver is ever greater than his conceptions yet ever remains one with his conception. For instance; before you are conscious of being man, you are first conscious of being. Then you become conscious of being man. Yet you remain as conceiver, greater than your conception—man.

Jesus discovered this glorious truth and declared himself to be one with God—not a God that man had fashioned. For he never recognized such a God. He said, "If any man should ever come, saying, 'Look here or look there,' believe them not, for the kingdom of God is within you." Heaven is within you. Therefore, when it is recorded that "He went unto his father," it is telling you that he rose in consciousness to the point where he was just conscious of being, thus transcending the limitations of his present conception of himself, called "Jesus."

In the awareness of being all things are possible, he said, "You shall decree a thing and it shall come to pass." This is his decreeing—rising in consciousness to the naturalness of being the thing desired. As he expressed it, "And I, if I be lifted up, I shall draw all men unto me." If I be lifted up in consciousness to the naturalness of the thing desired I will draw the manifestation of that desire unto me. For he states, "No man comes unto me save the father within me draws him, and I and my father are one." Therefore, consciousness is the father that is drawing the manifestations of life unto you.

You are, at this very moment, drawing into your world that which you are now conscious of being. Now you can see what is meant by, "You must be born again." If you are dissatisfied with your present expression in life the only way to change it, is to take your attention away from that which seems so real to you and rise in consciousness to that which you desire to be. You cannot serve two masters, therefore to take your attention from one state of consciousness and place it upon another is to die to one and live to the other.

The question, "Whom do you say that I AM?" is not addressed to a man called "Peter" by one called "Jesus." This is the eternal question addressed to one's self by one's true being. In other words, "Whom do you say that you are?" For your conviction of yourself—your opinion of yourself will determine your expression in life. He states, "You believe in God—believe also in me." In other words, it is the me within you that is this God.

Praying, then, is seen to be recognizing yourself to be that which you now desire, rather than its accepting form of petitioning a God that does not exist for that which you now desire.

So can't you see why the millions of prayers are unanswered? Men pray to a God that does not exist. For instance: To be conscious of being poor and to pray to a God for riches is to be rewarded with that which you are conscious of being—which is poverty. Prayers to be successful must be claiming rather than begging—so if you would pray for riches turn from your picture of poverty by denying the very evidence of your senses and assume the nature of being wealthy.

We are told, "When you pray go within in secret and shut the door. And that which your father sees in secret, with that will he reward you openly." We have identified the "father" to be the awareness of being. We have also identified the "door" to be the awareness of being. So "shutting the door" is shutting out that which "I" am now aware of being and claiming myself to be that which "I" desire to be. The very moment my claim is established to the point of conviction, that moment I begin to draw unto myself the evidence of my claim.

Do not question the how of these things appearing, for no man knows that way. That is, no manifestation knows how the things desired will appear.

Consciousness is the way or door through which things appear. He said, "I AM the way"—not "I," John Smith, am the way, but "I AM," the awareness of being, is the way through which the thing shall come. The signs always follow. They never precede. Things have no reality other than in consciousness. Therefore, get the consciousness first and the thing is compelled to appear.

You are told, "Seek ye first the kingdom of Heaven and all things shall be added unto you." Get first the consciousness of the things that you are seeking and leave the things alone. This is what is meant by "Ye shall decree a thing and it shall come to pass." Apply this principle and you will know what it is to "prove me and see." The story of Mary is the story of every man. Mary was not a woman—giving birth in some miraculous way to one called 'Jesus.' Mary is the awareness of being that ever remains virgin, no matter how many desires it gives birth to. Right now look upon yourself as this virgin Mary—being impregnated by yourself through the medium of desire—becoming one with your desire to the point of embodying or giving birth to your desire.

For instance: It is said of Mary (whom you now know to be yourself) that she know not a man. Yet she conceived. That is, you, John Smith, have no reason to believe that that which you now desire is possible, but having discovered your awareness of being to be God, you make this awareness your husband and conceive a man child (manifestation) of the Lord, "For thy maker is thine husband; the Lord of hosts is his name; the Lord God of the whole earth shall he be called." Your ideal or ambition is this conception—the first command to her, which is now to yourself, is "Go, tell no man." That is, do not discuss your ambitions or desires with another for the other will only echo your present fears. Secrecy is the first law to be observed in realizing your desire.

The second, as we are told in the story of Mary, is to "Magnify the Lord." We have identified the Lord as your awareness of being. Therefore, to "magnify the Lord" is to revalue or expand one's present conception of one's self to the point where this revaluation becomes natural. When this naturalness is attained you give birth by becoming that which you are one with in consciousness.

The story of creation is given us in digest form in the first chapter of John.

"In the beginning was the word." Now, this very second, is the "beginning" spoken of. It is the beginning of an urge—a desire. "The word" is the desire swimming around in your consciousness—seeking embodiment. The urge of itself has no reality, for "I AM" or the awareness of being is the only reality. Things live only as long as I AM aware of being them; so to realize one's desire, the second line of this first verse of John must be applied. That is, "And the word was with God." The word, or desire, must be fixed or united with consciousness to give it reality. The awareness becomes aware of being the thing desired, thereby nailing itself upon the form or conception—and giving life unto its conception—or resurrecting that which was heretofore a dead or unfulfilled desire. "Two shall agree as touching anything and it shall be established on earth."

This agreement is never made between two persons. It is between the awareness and the thing desired. You are now conscious of being, so you are actually saying to yourself, without using words, "I AM." Now, if it is a state of health that you are desirous of attaining, before you have any evidence of health in your world, you begin to FEEL yourself to be healthy. And the very second the feeling "I AM healthy" is attained the two have agreed. That is, I AM and health have agreed to be one and this agreement ever results in the birth of a child which is the thing agreed upon—in this case, health. And because I made the agreement I express the thing agreed. So you can see why Moses stated, "I AM hath sent me." For what being, other than I AM could send you into expression? None—for "I AM the way—Beside me there is no other." If you take the wings of the morning and fly into the uttermost parts of the world or if you make your bed in Hell, you will still be aware of being. You are ever sent into expression by your awareness and your expression is ever that which you are aware of being.

Again, Moses stated, "I AM that I AM." Now here is something to always bear in mind. You cannot put new wine in old bottles or new patches upon old garments. That is; you cannot take with you into the new consciousness any part of the old man. All of your present beliefs, fears and limitations are weights that bind you to your present level of consciousness. If you would transcend this level you must leave behind all that is now your present self, or conception of yourself. To do this you take your attention away from all that is now your problem or limitation and dwell upon just being. That is; you say silently but feeling to yourself, "I AM." Do not condition this "awareness" as yet. Just declare yourself to be, and continue to do so, until you are lost in the feeling of just being—faceless and form-less. When this expansion of consciousness is attained, then, within this formless deep of yourself give form to the new conception by FEELING yourself to be THAT which you desire to be.

You will find within this deep of yourself all things to be divinely possible. Everything in the world which you can conceive of being, is to you, within this present form-less awareness, a most natural attainment.

The invitation given us in the Scriptures is—"to be absent from the body and be present with the Lord." The "body" being your former conception of yourself and "the Lord"—your awareness of being. This is what is meant when Jesus said to Nicodemus, "Ye must be born again for except ye be born again ye cannot enter the kingdom of Heaven." That is; except you leave behind you your present conception of yourself and assume the nature of the new birth, you will continue to out-picture your present limitations.

The only way to change your expressions of life is to change your consciousness. For consciousness is the reality that eternally solidifies itself in the things round about you. Man's world in its every detail is his consciousness out-pictured. You can no more change your environment, or world, by destroying things than you can your reflection by destroying the mirror. Your environment, and all within it, reflects that which you are in consciousness. As long as you continue to be that in consciousness so long will you continue to out-picture it in your world.

Knowing this, begin to revalue yourself. Man has placed too little value upon himself. In the Book of Numbers you will read, "In that day there were giants in the land; and we were in our own sight as grasshoppers. And we were in their sight as grasshoppers." This does not mean a time in the dim past when man had the stature of giants. Today is the day—the eternal now—when conditions round about you have attained the appearance of giants (such as unemployed, the armies of your enemy, your problems and all things that seem to threaten you) those are the giants that make you feel yourself to be a grasshopper. But, you are told, you were first, in your own sight a grasshopper and because of this you were to the giants—a grasshopper. In other words, you can only be to others what you are first to yourself. Therefore, to revalue yourself and begin to feel yourself to be the giant, a center of power, is to dwarf these former giants and make of them grasshoppers. "All the inhabitants of the earth are as nothing, and he doeth according to his will in the armies of Heaven and among all the inhabitants of the earth; and none can stay his hand, nor say unto him, 'What doest thou'?" This being spoken of is not the orthodox God sitting in space but the one and only God—the everlasting father, your awareness of being. So awake to the power that you are, not as man, but as your true self, a faceless, formless awareness, and free yourself from your self-imposed prison.

"I am the good shepherd and know my sheep and am known of mine. My sheep hear my voice and I know them and they will follow me." Awareness is the good shepherd. What I am aware of being, is the "sheep" that follow me. So a good "shepherd" is your awareness that it has never lost one of the "sheep" that you are aware of being.

I am a voice calling in the wilderness of human confusion for such as I am aware of being, and never shall there come a time when that which I am convinced that I am shall fail to find me. "I AM" is an open door for all that I am to enter. Your awareness of being is lord and shepherd of your life. So, "The Lord is my shepherd; I shall not want" is seen in its true light now to be your consciousness. You could never be in want of proof or lack the evidence of that which you are aware of being.

This being true, why not become aware of being great; God-loving; wealthy; healthy; and all attributes that you admire?

It is just as easy to possess the consciousness of these qualities as it is to possess their opposites for you have not your present consciousness because of your world. On the contrary, your world is what it is because of your present consciousness. Simple, is it not? Too simple in fact for the wisdom of man that tries to complicate everything.

Paul said of this principle, "It is to the Greeks" (or wisdom of this world) "foolishness." "And to the Jews" (or those who look for signs) "a stumbling block"; with the result, that man continues to walk in darkness rather than awake to the being that he is. Man has so long worshipped the images of his own making that at first he finds this revelation blasphemous, since it spells death to all his previous beliefs in a God apart from himself. This revelation will bring the knowledge that "I and my father are one but my father is greater than I." You are one with your present conception of yourself. But you are greater than that which you are at present aware of being.

Before man can attempt to transform his world he must first lay the foundation—"I AM the Lord." That is, man's awareness, his consciousness of being is God. Until this is firmly established so that no suggestion or argument put forward by others can shake it, he will find himself returning to the slavery of his former beliefs. "If ye believe not that I AM he, ye shall die in your sins." That is, you shall continue to be confused and thwarted until you find the cause of your confusion. When you have lifted up the son of man then shall you know that I AM he, that is, that I, John Smith, do nothing of myself, but my father, or that state of consciousness which I am now one with does the works.

When this is realized every urge and desire that springs within you shall find expression in your world. "Behold I stand at the door and knock. If any man hear my voice and open the door I will come in to him and sup with him and he with me." The "I" knocking at the door is the urge.

The door is your consciousness. To open the door is to become one with that which is knocking by FEEL-ING oneself to be the thing desired. To feel one's desire as impossible is to shut the door or deny this urge expression. To rise in consciousness to the naturalness of the thing felt is to swing wide the door and invite this one into embodiment.

That is why it is constantly recorded that Jesus left the world of manifestation and ascended unto his father. Jesus, as you and I, found all things impossible to Jesus, as man. But having discovered his father to be the state of consciousness of the thing desired, he but left behind him the "Jesus consciousness" and rose in consciousness to that state desired and stood upon it until he became one with it. As he made himself one with that, he became that in expression.

This is Jesus' simple message to man: Men are but garments that the impersonal being, I AM—the presence that men call God—dwells in. Each garment has certain limitations. In order to transcend these limitations and give expression to that which, as man—John Smith—you find yourself incapable of doing, you take your attention away from your present limitations, or John Smith conception of yourself, and merge yourself in the feeling of being that which you desire. Just how this desire or newly attained consciousness will embody itself, no man knows. For I, or the newly attained consciousness, has ways that ye know not of; its ways are past finding out. Do not speculate as to the HOW of this consciousness embodying itself, for no man is wise enough to know the how. Speculation is proof that you have not attained to the naturalness of being the thing desired and so are filled with doubts.

You are told, "He who lacks wisdom let him ask of God, that gives to all liberally, and upbraideth not; and it shall be given unto him. But let him ask not doubting for he who doubts is as a wave of the sea that is tossed and battered by the winds. And let not such a one think that he shall receive anything from the Lord." You can see why this statement is made, for only upon the rock of faith can anything be established. If you have not the consciousness of the thing you have not the cause or foundation upon which the thing is erected.

A proof of this established consciousness is given you in the words, "Thank you, father." When you come into the joy of thanksgiving so that you actually feel grateful for having received that which is not yet apparent to the senses, you have definitely become one in consciousness with the thing for which you gave thanks. God (your awareness) is not mocked. You are ever receiving that which you are aware of being and no man gives thanks for something which he has not received. "Thank you father" is not, as it is used by many today, a sort of magical formula. You need never utter aloud the words, "Thank you, father." In applying this principle as you rise in consciousness to the point where you are really grateful and happy for having received the thing desired, you automatically rejoice and give thanks inwardly. You have already accepted the gift which was but a desire before you rose in consciousness, and your faith is now the substance that shall clothe your desire.

This rising in consciousness is the spiritual marriage where two shall agree upon being one and their likeness or image is established on earth.

"For whatsoever ye ask in my name the same give I unto you." "Whatsoever" is quite a large measure. It is the unconditional. It does not state if society deems it right or wrong that you should ask it, it rests with you. Do you really want it? Do you desire it? That is all that is necessary. Life will give it to you if you ask "in his name."

His name is not a name that you pronounce with the lips. You can ask forever in the name of God or Jehovah or Christ Jesus and you will ask in vain. "Name" means nature; so, when you ask in the nature of a thing, results ever follow. To ask in the name is to rise in consciousness and become one in nature with the thing desired, rise in consciousness to the nature of the thing, and you will become that thing in expression. Therefore, "what things so ever ye desire, when ye pray, believe that ye receive them and ye shall receive them."

Praying, as we have shown you before, is recognition— the injunction to believe that ye receive is first person, present tense. This means that you must be in the nature of the things asked for before you can receive them.

To get into the nature easily, general amnesty is necessary. We are told, "Forgive if ye have aught against any, that your father also, which is in Heaven, may forgive you. But if ye forgive not, neither will your father forgive you." This may seem to be some personal God who is pleased or displeased with your actions but this is not the case.

Consciousness, being God, if you hold in consciousness anything against man, you are binding that condition in your world. But to release man from all condemnation is to free yourself so that you may rise to any level necessary; there is, therefore, no condemnation to those in Christ Jesus.

Therefore, a very good practice before you enter into your meditation is first to free every man in the world from blame. For LAW is never violated and you can rest confidently in the knowledge that every man's conception of himself is going to be his reward. So you do not have to bother yourself about seeing whether or not man gets what you consider he should get. For life makes no mistakes and always gives man that which man first gives himself.

This brings us to that much abused statement of the Bible on tithing. Teachers of all kinds have enslaved man with this affair of tithing, for not themselves understanding the nature of tithing and being themselves fearful of lack, they have led their followers to believe that a tenth part of their income should be given to the Lord. Meaning, as they make very clear, that, when one gives a tenth part of his income to their particular organization he is giving his "tenth part" to the Lord—(or is tithing). But remember, "I AM the Lord." Your awareness of being is the God that you give to and you ever give in this manner.

Therefore when you claim yourself to be anything, you have given that claim or quality to God. And your awareness of being, which is no respecter of persons, will return to you pressed down, shaken together, and running over with that quality or attribute which you claim for yourself.

Awareness of being is nothing that you could ever name. To claim God to be rich; to be great; to be love; to be all wise; is to define that which cannot be defined. For God is nothing that could ever be named.

Tithing is necessary and you do tithe with God. But from now on give to the only God and see to it that you give him the quality that you desire as man to express by claiming yourself to be the great, the wealthy, the loving, the all wise.

Do not speculate as to how you shall express these qualities or claims, for life has a way that you, as man, know not of. Its ways are past finding out. But, I assure you, the day you claim these qualities to the point of conviction, your claims will be honored. There is nothing covered that shall not be uncovered. That which is spoken in secret shall be proclaimed from the housetops. That is, your secret convictions of yourself—these secret claims that no man knows of, when really believed, will be shouted from the housetops in your world. For your convictions of yourself are the words of the God within you, which words are spirit and cannot return unto you void but must accomplish whereunto they are sent.

You are at this moment calling out of the infinite that which you are now conscious of being. And not one word or conviction will fail to find you.

"I AM the vine and ye are the branches." Consciousness is the "vine," and those qualities which you are now conscious of being are as "branches" that you feed and keep alive. Just as a branch has no life except it be rooted in the vine, so likewise things have no life except you be conscious of them. Just as a branch withers and dies if the sap of the vine ceases to flow towards it, so do things in your world pass away if you take your attention from them, because your attention is as the sap of life that keeps alive and sustains the things of your world.

To dissolve a problem that now seems so real to you all that you do is remove your attention from it. In spite of its seeming reality, turn from it in consciousness. Become indifferent and begin to feel yourself to be that which would be the solution of the problem.

For instance; if you were imprisoned no man would have to tell you that you should desire freedom. Freedom, or rather the desire of freedom, would be automatic. So why look behind the four walls of your prison bars? Take your attention from being imprisoned and begin to feel yourself to be free. FEEL it to the point where it is natural—the very second you do so, those prison bars will dissolve. Apply this same principle to any problem.

I have seen people who were in debt up to their ears apply this principle and in the twinkling of an eye debts that were mountainous were removed. I have seen those whom doctors had given up as incurable take their attention away from their problem of disease and begin to feel themselves to be well in spite of the evidence of their sense to the contrary. In no time at all this so called "incurable disease" vanished and left no scar.

Your answer to, "Whom do you say that I AM"? ever determines your expression. As long as you are conscious of being imprisoned or diseased, or poor, so long will you continue to out-picture or express these conditions.

When man realized that he is now that which he is seeking and begins to claim that he is, he will have the proof of his claim. This cue is given you in words, "Whom seek ye?" And they answered, "Jesus." And the voice said, "I am he." "Jesus" here means salvation or savior. You are seeking to be salvaged from that which is not your problem.

"I am" is he that will save you. If you are hungry, your savior is food. If you are poor, your savior is riches. If you are imprisoned, your savior is freedom. If you are diseased, it will not be a man called Jesus who will save you, but health will become your savior. Therefore, claim "I am he," in other words, claim yourself to be the thing desired. Claim it in consciousness—not in words—and consciousness will reward you with your claim. You are told, "You shall find me when you FEEL after me." Well, FEEL after that quality in consciousness until you FEEL yourself to be it. When you lose yourself in the feeling of being it, the quality will embody itself in your world.

You are healed from your problem when you touch the solution of it. "Who has touched me? For I perceive virtue is gone out of me." Yes, the day you touch this being within you—FEELING yourself to be cured or healed, virtues will come out of your very self and solidify themselves in your world as healings.

It is said, "You believe in God. Believe also in me for I am he." Have the faith of God. "He made himself one with God and found it not robbery to do the works of God." Go you and do likewise. Yes, begin to believe your awareness, your consciousness of being to be God. Claim for yourself all the attributes that you have heretofore given an external God and you will begin to express these claims.

"For I am not a God afar off. I am nearer than your hands and feet—nearer than your very breathing." I am your awareness of being. I am that in which all that I shall ever be aware of being shall begin and end. "For before the world was I AM; and when the world shall cease to be, I AM; before Abraham was, I AM." This I AM is your awareness. "Except the Lord build the house they labor in vain that build it." "The Lord," being your consciousness, except that which you seek is first established in your consciousness, you will labor in vain to find it. All things must begin and end in consciousness.

So, blessed indeed is the man that trusteth in himself—for man's faith in God will ever be measured by his confidence in himself. You believe in a God, believe also in ME.

Put not your trust in men for men but reflect the being that you are, and can only bring to you or do unto you that which you have first done unto yourself.

"No man taketh away my life, I lay it down myself." I have the power to lay it down and the power to take it up again.

No matter what happens to man in this world it is never an accident. It occurs under the guidance of an exact and changeless Law.

"No man" (manifestation) "comes unto me except the father within me draw him," and "I and my father are one." Believe this truth and you will be free. Man has always blamed others for that which he is and will continue to do so until he find himself as cause of all. "I AM" comes not to destroy but to fulfill. "I AM," the awareness within you, destroys nothing but ever fills full the molds or conception one has of one's self.

It is impossible for the poor man to find wealth in this world no matter how he is surrounded with it until he first claims himself to be wealthy. For signs follow, they do not precede. To constantly kick and complain against the limitations of poverty while remaining poor in consciousness is to play the fool's game. Changes cannot take place from that level of consciousness for life is constantly out-picturing all levels.

Follow the example of the prodigal son. Realize that you, yourself, brought about this condition of waste and lack and make the decision within yourself to rise to a higher level where the fatted calf, the ring, and the robe await your claim.

There was no condemnation of the prodigal when he had the courage to claim this inheritance as his own. Others will condemn us only as long as we continue in that for which we condemn ourselves. So: "Happy is the man that condemneth himself not in that which he alloweth." For to life nothing is condemned. All is expressed.

Life does not care whether you call yourself rich or poor; strong or weak. It will eternally reward you with that which you claim as true of yourself.

The measurements of right and wrong belong to man alone. To life there is nothing right or wrong. As Paul stated in his letters to the Romans: "I know and am persuaded by the Lord Jesus that there is nothing unclean of itself, but to him that esteemeth anything to be unclean, to him it is unclean." Stop asking yourself whether you are worthy or unworthy to receive that which you desire. You, as man, did not create the desire. Your desires are ever fashioned within you because of what you now claim yourself to be.

When a man is hungry, (without thinking) he automatically desires food. When imprisoned, he automatically desires freedom and so forth. Your desires contain within themselves the plan of self-expression.

So leave all judgments out of the picture and rise in consciousness to the level of your desire and make yourself one with it by claiming it to be so now. For: "My grace is sufficient for thee. My strength is made in weakness."

Have faith in this unseen claim until the conviction is born within you that it is so. Your confidence in this claim will pay great rewards. Just a little while and he, the thing desired, will come. But without faith it is impossible to realize anything. Through faith the worlds were framed because "faith is the substance of the thing hoped for—the evidence of the thing not yet seen."

Don't be anxious or concerned as to results. They will follow just as surely as day follows night.

Look upon your desires—all of them—as the spoken words of God, and every word or desire a promise. The reason most of us fail to realize our desires is because we are constantly conditioning them. Do not condition your desire. Just accept it as it comes to you. Give thanks for it to the point that you are grateful for having already received it—then go about your way in peace.

Such acceptance of your desire is like dropping seed—
fertile seed—into prepared soil. For when you can drop
the thing desired in consciousness, confident that it shall
appear, you have done all that is expected of you. But, to
be worried or concerned about the HOW of your desire
maturing is to hold these fertile seeds in a mental grasp,
and, therefore, never to have dropped them in the soil of
confidence.

The reason men condition their desires is because they
constantly judge after the appearance of being and see the
things as real—forgetting that the only reality is the consciousness back of them.

To see things as real is to deny that all things are possible to God. The man who is imprisoned and sees his four
walls as real is automatically denying the urge or promise
of God within him of freedom.

A question often asked when this statement is made is;
If one's desire is a gift of God how can you say that if one
desires to kill a man that such a desire is good and therefore God sent? In answer to this let me say that no man
desires to kill another. What he does desire is to be freed
from such a one. But because he does not believe that the
desire to be free from such a one contains within itself the
powers of freedom, he conditions that desire and sees the
only way to express such freedom is to destroy the man—
forgetting that the life wrapped within the desire has ways

that he, as man, knows not of. Its ways are past finding out. Thus man distorts the gifts of God through his lack of faith.

Problems are the mountains spoken of that can be removed if one has but the faith of a grain of a mustard seed. Men approach their problem as did the old lady who, on attending service and hearing the priest say, "If you had but the faith of a grain of a mustard seed you would say unto yonder mountain 'be thou removed' and it shall be removed and nothing is impossible to you." That night as she said her prayers, she quoted this part of the Scriptures and retired to bed in what she thought was faith. On arising in the morning she rushed to the window and exclaimed:

For this is how man approaches his problem. He knows that they are still going to confront him. And because life is no respecter of persons and destroys nothing, it continues to keep alive that which he is conscious of being.

Things will disappear only as man changes in consciousness. Deny it if you will, it still remains a fact that consciousness is the only reality and things but mirror that which you are in consciousness. So the heavenly state you are seeking will be found only in consciousness, for the kingdom of heaven is within you. As the will of heaven is ever done on earth you are today living in the heaven that you have established within you. For here on this very earth your heaven reveals itself. The kingdom of heaven really is at hand. NOW is the accepted time. So create a new heaven, enter into a new state of consciousness and a new earth will appear.

"The former things shall pass away. They shall not be remembered nor come into mind any more. For behold, I, come quickly and my reward is with me."

I am nameless but will take upon myself every name (nature) that you call me. Remember it is you, yourself, that I speak of as "me." So every conception that you have of yourself—that is every deep conviction—you have of yourself is that which you shall appear as being—for I AM not fooled; God is not mocked. Now let me instruct you in the art of fishing. It is recorded that the disciples fished all night and caught nothing. Then Jesus came upon the scene and told them to cast their nets in once more, into the same waters that only a moment before were barren— and this time their nets were bursting with the catch.

This story is taking place in the world today right within you, the reader. For you have within you all the elements necessary to go fishing. But until you find that Jesus Christ (your awareness) is Lord, you will fish, as did these disciples, in the night of human darkness. That is, you will fish for THINGS thinking things to be real and will fish with the human bait—which is a struggle and an effort— trying to make contact with this one and that one: trying to coerce this being or the other being; and all such effort will be in vain. But when you discover your awareness of being to be Christ Jesus you will let him direct your fishing. And you will fish in consciousness for the things that you desire. For your desire will be the fish that you will catch, because your consciousness is the only living reality you will fish in the deep waters of consciousness.

If you would catch that which is beyond your present capacity you must launch out into deeper waters, for, within your present consciousness such fish or desires cannot swim. To launch out into deeper waters, you leave behind you all that is now your present problem, or limitation, by taking your ATTENTION AWAY from it. Turn your back completely upon every problem and limitation that you now possess.

Dwell upon just being by saying, "I AM," "I AM," "I AM," to yourself. Continue to declare to yourself that you just are. Do not condition this declaration, just continue to FEEL yourself to be and without warning you will find yourself slipping the anchor that tied you to the shallow of your problems and moving out into the deep.

This is usually accompanied with the feeling of expansion. You will FEEL yourself expand as though you were actually growing. Don't be afraid, for courage is necessary. You are not going to die to anything by your former limitations, but they are going to die as you move away from them, for they live only in your consciousness. In this deep or expanded consciousness you will find yourself to be a power that you had never dreamt of before. The things desired before you shoved off from the shores of limitation are the fish you are going to catch in this deep. Because you have lost all consciousness of your problems and barriers, it is now the easiest thing in the world to FEEL yourself to be one with the things desired.

Because I AM (your consciousness) is the resurrection and the life, you must attach this resurrecting power that you are to the thing desired if you would make it appear and live in your world. Now you begin to assume the nature of the thing desired by feeling, "I AM wealthy"; "I AM free"; "I AM strong." When these "FEELS" are fixed within yourself, your formless being will take upon itself the forms of the things felt. You become 'crucified' upon the feelings of wealth, freedom, and strength. Remain buried in the stillness of these convictions. Then, as a thief in the night and when you least expect it, these qualities will be resurrected in your world as living realities.

The world shall touch you and see that you are flesh and blood for you shall begin to bear fruit of the nature of these qualities newly appropriated. This is the art of successful fishing for the manifestations of life.

Successful realization of the thing desired is also told us in the story of Daniel in the lion's den. Here, it is recorded that Daniel, while in the lion's den, turned his back upon the lions and looked towards the light coming from above; that the lions remained powerless and Daniel's faith in his God saved him.

This also is your story and you too must do as Daniel did. If you found yourself in a lion's den you would have no other concern but lions. You would not be thinking of one thing in the world but your problem—which problem would be lions.

Yet, you are told that Daniel turned his back upon them and looked towards the light that was his God. If we would follow the example of Daniel we would, while imprisoned within the den of poverty or sickness, take our attention away from our problems of debts or sickness and dwell upon the thing we seek.

If we do not look back in consciousness to our problems but continue in faith—believing ourselves to be that which we seek, we too will find our prison walls open and the thing sought—yes, "whatsoever things"—realized.

Another story is told us; of the widow and the three drops of oil. The prophet asked the widow, "What have ye in your house?" And she replied, "Three drops of oil." He then said to her, "Go borrow vessels. Close the door after ye have returned into your house and begin to pour." And she poured from three drops of oil into all the borrowed vessels, filling them to capacity with oil remaining.

You, the reader, are this widow. You have not a husband to impregnate you or make you fruitful, for a "widow" is a barren state. Your awareness is now the Lord—or the prophet that has become your husband.

Follow the example of the widow, who instead of recognizing an emptiness or nothingness, recognized the something—three drops of oil.

Then the command to her, "Go within and close the door," that is, shut the door of the senses that tell you of the empty measures, the debts, the problems.

When you have taken your attention away completely by shutting out the evidence of the senses, begin to FEEL the joy—(symbolized by oil)—of having received the things desired. When the agreement is established within you so that all doubts and fears have passed away, then, you too will fill all the empty measures of your life and will have an abundance running over. Recognition is the power that conjures in the world. Every state that you have ever recognized, you have embodied. That which you are recognizing as true of yourself today is that which you are experiencing. So be as the widow and recognize joy, no matter how little the beginnings of recognition, and you will be generously rewarded—for the world is a magnified mirror, magnifying everything that you are conscious of being.

"I AM the Lord the God, which has brought thee out of the land of Egypt, out of the house of bondage; thou shalt have no other gods before me." What a glorious revelation, your awareness now revealed as the Lord thy God! Come, awake from your dream of being imprisoned. Realize that the earth is yours, "and the fullness thereof; the world, and all that dwells therein."

You have become so enmeshed in the belief that you are man that you have forgotten the glorious being that you are. Now with your memory restored DECREE the unseen to appear and it SHALL appear, for all things are compelled to respond to the Voice of God, Your awareness of being—the world is AT YOUR COMMAND!

II

CHARIOT OF FIRE: THE IDEAS OF NEVILLE GODDARD

By Mitch Horowitz

This was my first public talk on Neville, delivered June 28, 2013, at the now-defunct arts space Observatory in Gowanus, Brooklyn. It includes the complete talk and the question-and-answer session that followed. —MH

Some of you know my work, my book *Occult America*, and things that I've done related to that. *Occult America* is a history of supernatural religious movements in our country. A few of you who know my work are aware that I feel strongly that occult, esoteric, and metaphysical movements have touched this country very deeply. I write about these movements not only as a historian who is passionately interested in how the paranormal, occult, and supernatural have influenced our religion, our economy, our psychology, and our views of ourselves; but I also write about these things as a participant, as a kind of a believing historian. I do not view occult thought movements strictly as historical phenomena, which may reveal aspects of human nature; that's true enough, but I think that within the folds of such movements there exist actual ideas for human transformation.

I don't believe in looking into philosophies simply in order to place them in museum cases and to label them. Rather, I think we need practical philosophies that contribute to real-life transformation in the here and now. In my study of different occult and mystical systems, some of which I wrote about in *Occult America* and some of which I'm writing about in my next book *One Simple Idea*, I must tell you the most impactful, elegant, simplest, and dramatically powerful figure I have come across is Neville Goddard.

He was born to an Anglican family on the island of Barbados in 1905. It was a family of ten children, nine boys and one girl. Neville came here to New York City to study theater in 1922. He had some success and also fell into a variety of mystical and occult philosophies. Neville eventually came to feel that he had discovered the master key to existence. Up to this point in my experiments, I conclude: he may have been right.

You can determine that for yourself, because I'm going to start off this presentation by giving you his system. I am also going to provide some history: where he came from, who his teachers were, what his ideas grew out of, who he has influenced, and why he proved vastly ahead of his time. Some of the methods and ideas that Neville experimented with are being heard about today through unsensationalized discussions of developments in quantum physics and neurobiology.

I will also consider the possible identity of the hidden spiritual master named Abdullah who Neville said was his teacher in New York City. Are there spiritual masters, masters of wisdom in the world? Are there beings who can provide help to us when we sincerely desire it? Is that a real possibility or is that just fantasy? I think it's a possibility. It may have played out in his existence.

But we're really here to talk about the practical side of his philosophy. There are many interesting figures who I reference in this talk—dramatic figures whose lives spanned the globe. But we're talking about Neville *because of the usefulness of his ideas* and I want to start with that.

MIND AS GOD

Neville believed very simply in the principle that your imagination is God, the human imagination is God, and that Scripture and all the stories from Scripture, both Old Testament and New Testament, have absolutely no basis in historical reality. The entire book is a metaphor, a blueprint for the individual's personal development. In particular, the New Testament tells the story of God symbolically, of God descending into human form, of humanity becoming asleep to its own divine essence or Christ essence, and believing itself to live within a coarse, limited world of material parameters, of then being crucified and experiencing the agony of his forgetfulness. Christ yells out in the across, "My God, my God, why hast thou forsaken me?" The individual is then resurrected into the realization of his or her divine potentiality, which is the birthright of every individual.

Neville maintained, through his reading of Scripture, his personal probing as a philosopher, and his experiments as an individual, that there is no God outside of the creative powers of the imagination; and that those who wrote Scripture never intended to communicate that there was a God outside of the individual's imagination. The creative force within us—which thinks, plans, pictures, ponders, and falls in and out of emotive states—is symbolically represented in Scripture as God.

Neville maintained that your thoughts, your mental pictures, and your emotive states create your concrete reality—and do at every moment of existence. We are oblivious and asleep to this fact. We live in these coarse shells, we suffer, we cry, we have fleeting joys, we leave these forms. We go through life in a state of slumber without ever knowing that each one of us is a physical form in which creation is experiencing itself. We eventually come to the realization through our causative minds we can experience the powers written about in symbolically in the New Testament and embodied as the story of Christ resurrected.

I want to say to you that Neville meant all of this in the most radical and literal sense. There was nothing inexact or qualified in what he said. He took a radical stand and he continually put up a challenge to his audiences: *try it*. Try it tonight and if it doesn't work, discard me, discard my philosophy, prove me a liar. He sold nothing. He published a handful of books, most of which are now public domain. He gave lectures Grateful Dead-style where he allowed everybody to tape record them and distribute them freely, which is why his talks are now all over the Internet. There's nothing to join. There's nothing to buy. There's no copyright holder. There's just this man and his ideas.

THREE-STEP MIRACLE

Neville's outlook can be reduced to a three-part formula, which is incredibly simple, but also requires commitment.

First, every creative act begins with an absolute, passionate desire. It sounds so easy, doesn't it? We walk around all day long with desires; I want this, I want that, I want money, I want relationships, I want this person to pay attention to me, I want this attainment. But look again. We often have superficial understandings of our desires and we're dishonest about our desires.

We're dishonest about our desires because we don't want to say to ourselves, in our innermost thoughts, *what we really want.* Sometimes we're repulsed by our desires, and that's the truth. We live in a society that's filled with so much personal license and freedom on the surface, of course, but we often don't want to acknowledge things to ourselves that maybe we believe aren't attractive.

I want to tell a personal story and I want to be very personal with you because I'm talking to you about a man and a philosophy that is enormously challenging and practical, if you really take it seriously. I have no right to be standing here talking to you unless I tell you about some of my own experiences. I want to tell you about one of my personal experiences as it relates to this first point: *desire.* Years ago, I knew a woman who was a psychic. A nationally known person, somebody I assume some of you have heard of, not household name maybe, but well known. I thought she had a genuine psychical gift. I thought she had something.

Yet I didn't like the way she led her life because I thought, personally, that she could be a violent person—not physically violent but emotionally; she would manipulate people around her, bully people, push people around. I didn't really like her but I did feel that she had a true gift. One night I was talking to her. We were on a parking lot somewhere having conversation, and she stopped. She said to me, "You know what you want? You want power. But your problem is that you have an overdeveloped super-ego." As soon as I heard this I wanted to push it away. And I spent years pushing it away. Years pushing it away because I thought to myself, "Well, I don't want power like you. I don't want power to push people around, to bully people, to be violent towards people. I don't want that, no." So I recoiled from what she said. But it haunted me. It haunted me. I could never get away from it.

You don't know really what haunts you until you confront something in yourself, or maybe something that a sensitive person says to you, which leaves the terrible impression that they might just may be speaking the truth. So when Neville talks about desire, he's not talking about something superficial that we keep telling ourselves day after day. He really wants you to get down into the guts of things, where you might want something that makes you very uncomfortable. There are ways we don't like to see ourselves. But Neville maintains that desire is the voice of the God within you; and to walk away from it is to walk away from the potential greatness within yourself. Desire is the language of God. Neville means this in the most literal sense.

The second step is physical immobility. This is the part where you actually do something. You enter a physically immobile state. Choose the time of day when you like to meditate, whether it's early morning, whether it's late at night. The time of day Neville chose was 3:00 p.m. He would finish lunch, settle into an easy chair, and go into a drowsy state. Now, this is very important because we think of meditation typically as a state of exquisite awareness. We don't think of meditation as drowsiness. People use these terms in different ways. Neville believed—and as I will talk about this later in this presentation—that the mind is uniquely powerful and suggestible in its drowsy state, hovering just before sleep, but not yet crossing into sleep. It is a controlled reverie. Or a cognizant dream state. Sleep researchers call this hypnagogia. You enter it twice daily: at night when you're drifting off and in the morning when you're coming to (this is sometimes called hypnopompia).

Our minds are exquisitely sensitive at such times. People who suffer from depression or grief describe their early morning hours as the most difficult time of day. The reason for that, I'm convinced, is that it is a time when our rational defenses are down. We're functioning almost entirely from emotion. We are conscious but we are also in this very subtle, fine state between sleep and wakefulness, and our rational defenses are slackened. Let me tell you something vital—and I can attest to this from personal experience. If you are trying to solve a personal problem, do not do it at 5:00 in the morning. Do not.

Your rational defenses are down when you need them most.

When you need your your intellect, whether you're solving a financial problem, whether you're going through a relationship problem, whatever it is, do not use the time of day when it is at its lowest ebb. At 5 a.m. your mind isn't fully working. Your emotions are working. It is a tough, tough time to deal with problems. But it is a very unique time to deal with desires—and for the same reason. When your rational defenses are down, your mind can go in remarkable directions.

I'm going to talk later about developments in psychical research, where there are some extraordinary findings under rigorous clinical conditions, in which people are induced into this hypnagogic state, the state between sleep and wakefulness, and the mind can evince remarkable abilities.

So, Neville said to enter this state of physical immobility. You can most easily do it just before you go to sleep at night. He didn't say do it when you wake up in the morning but I think you can extrapolate that that works, too. You can also do it when you're meditating. You can do it whenever you want. It takes only a few minutes, but go into a very relaxed bodily state or just let yourself be taken into it naturally when you go to bed at night.

And now *the third step*: form a very clear, simple mental scene that would naturally occur following the fulfilment of your desire. Keep it very simple. Run it through your head as long as it feels natural.

A woman attended one of Neville's lectures in Los Angeles and told him simply that she wanted to be married. He told her to enact the mental feeling of a wedding band on her finger. Just that. Keep it very simple. Mentally feel the weight and pressure of the ring on your finger. Maybe feel yourself spinning it around on your finger. Maybe there's something you want from an individual. Select an act that seems simple. Just a handshake, perhaps. Something that communicates that you received something—recognition, a promotion, a congratulation.

You must picture yourself *within* the scene. You must see from within the scene. Don't see yourself doing something as though you're watching it on a screen. Neville was adamant about this. He would say, "If I want to imagine myself climbing a ladder, I don't *see* myself climbing a ladder. *I climb.*" You must feel hands on the ladder. Feel your weight was you step up each rung. You are not watching the scene—you are in it.

Whatever it is, find one simple, clear, persuasive, physical action that would communicate the attainment of your goal, and think from that end, think from the end of the goal fulfilled. Run this through your mind as long as it feels natural.

Neville would always say, "When you open your eyes, you'll be back here in the coarse world that you might not want to be in, but if you persist in this, your assumption will harden into fact." You may wake up, come out of your physical immobility, and discover that the world remains exactly as it was. If you want to be in Paris and you open your eyes in New York, you may be disappointed. Keep doing it and extraordinary events will unfold to secure precisely what you have pictured in your mind. Persistence is key.

USING THE EMOTIONS

Now, I want to emphasize one aspect of Neville's philosophy, which I feel that he could have gone further in explaining, and that is the necessity of your visual scene being accompanied by the attendant emotional state. We often make the mistake in the positive-mind movement of equating thought with emotions. They are different things. I have a physical existence. I have intellectual existence. I have an emotional existence. Part of why you may feel torn apart when approaching mind causation is that all of these aspects of your existence—the physical, the mental, and the emotional—are going their own way, running on separate tracks. You may vow not to eat, and you may mean it, but the body wants to eat—and next thing you know the body is in control. You may vow not to get angry—but the emotions take over and you fly into rage. You may think, "I am going to use my intellect and not my passions"—but the passions rule your action. These three forces, body, mind, and intellect, have their own lives—and intellect is the weakest among them. Otherwise we wouldn't struggle with addictions or violent outbursts or impulsive actions. But we find that we are pieces.

This presents a challenge. Because when you enact your mental scene of fulfillment, you also must attain the emotive state that you would feel in your fulfillment. When you approach this teaching you benefit from being a kind of actor or thespian, as Neville was early in his career. Method Acting is a good exercise for enacting this method. Read Stanislavski's *An Actor Prepares*. Anybody who's been trained in Method Acting often learns to use a kind of inner monologue to get themselves into an emotional state. That's a good exercise. You must get the emotions in play.

Let's say you want a promotion at work. You could picture your boss saying to you, "Congratulations—well done!" You must try to feel the emotions that you would feel in that state. Hypnagogia can also help with this because, as noted, the rational defenses are lowered and the mind is more suggestible.

To review Neville's formula: 1) Identify an intense and sincere desire. 2) Enter a state of physical immobility, i.e., the drowsy hypnagogic state. 3) Gently run a scene through your mind that would occur if your wish was ful-filled. Let it be an emotional experience.

HOW IT HAPPENED

I want to tell another personal story. Neville always chal-lenged his listeners: "Test it. Test it. What do you most desire right now? Go home this night and test it. Prove me wrong," he would say. I decided to test him and I want to give you the example. It is recent to this talk, explicit, and absolutely real.

In addition to being a writer, I'm a publisher. I'm the editor-in-chief of a division of Penguin that publishes New Age and metaphysical books. After considerable effort to locate the descendants of the author, I acquired the rights to republish a 1936 self-help book called *Wake Up and Live!* by Dorothea Brande. In this book, Brande writes that the pathology of human nature is what she called a *will to fail*. We fear failure and humiliation more than we crave success, so we constantly sabotage our plans in order to avoid the possibility of failure. We procrastinate. We make excuses. We blow important due dates or wreck professional rela-tionships because we're more frightened of failure than we are hungry for success. But Brande further believed that if you were to *act as though it were impossible to fail*, you could bypass this self-negating pattern and achieve great things.

As mentioned, I spent a year trying to find her descendants so I could buy rights to this book, and I finally did. After this effort, I learned of an audio publisher who wanted to issue out an audio edition. I do a lot of audio narration, although I was still just getting started at this point, and I told this publisher that I was eager to narrate this book. I had recorded for this publisher before. It had been successful and I thought, naturally they'll agree. But they wouldn't get back to me. My e-mails were ignored. My phone calls were ignored. I was very frustrated. I couldn't understand why they wouldn't want me to do this book. I was obviously brimming of passion for it. I had done good work before. But I just couldn't get anywhere. I was totally stuck. I was very frustrated. Finally the publisher replied to me with a decisive, "No."

I thought to myself, "Well, not only do I want to be doing more audiobooks, but this is the kind of book that I was born to read." I went into this exercise and I formed a mental picture. I'm not going to tell you what it was. It was too personal but it was also very simple. I formed a mental picture. I reviewed it faithfully two or three times a day for about two weeks.

Out of the clear blue, without any outer intervention on my part, a rights manager called to say, "Guess what?

Someone else actually just bought the rights to that book. It's not with that audio publisher anymore. There's been a change. There's a new audio publisher." I said, "Please tell that new publisher that I am dying to read this book." She got back to me. The new publisher said, "I sent Horowitz an e-mail a week ago asking him to read another audiobook and he never get back to me." I had gotten no such email. I went into my spam folder and found nothing. I went into a still deeper spam filter—and there is was. We signed a deal for me to narrate a total of three books, including *Wake Up and Live!*

I went from being ignored, to being told no, to signing a three-book narration deal. That relationship became one of the most central of my professional life. That same publisher issued this book that you are now reading. I did nothing to influence any of this in the outer world. I didn't do anything or contact anybody. I just did my visualization as Neville prescribed. It ended with the new audio publisher saying, "I contacted him a week ago. Why didn't he get back to me?"

For various reasons, this episode could be considered ordinary and I'm not oblivious to that. But I can say the following: from where I stood, and from long experience, it did not appear ordinary. "Take my challenge and put my words to the test. If the law does not work, its knowledge will not comfort you, and if it is not true, you must discard it. I hope you will be bold enough to test me" That's what Neville said over and over. You don't have to join anything. You don't have to buy anything. You can go online and listen to his lectures. Many of his books can be downloaded for free. His lectures can be downloaded for free. All he would insist is: "Put me to the test. Put me to the test."

ECCE HOMO

Neville was born in 1905 on the island of Barbados, as mentioned. He was not born to a wealthy, land-holding family. He was born to an Anglican family of merchants. He was one of ten children, nine boys and a girl. The family ran a food service and catering business, which later mushroomed into a highly profitable corporation. One of the things that I found about Neville is that the life details and events he claimed in his lectures often turned out to be verifiably true.

I've done a lot of work to track down and verify some of Neville's claims. He came to New York City to study theater and dancing in 1922. He didn't have any money. He was a poor kid and knocked about. He lived in a shared apartment on the Upper West Side on West 75th Street. His large family back home was not rich but over the course of time, they became very rich. They later put him on kind of an allowance or a monthly stipend. Much later, he was able to pursue his studies into the occult, into philosophy, into mysticism, completely independently.

Goddard Industries is today a major catering business in Barbados. They not only cater parties and events, but they cater for airlines. They cater for cruise ships and industrial facilities. By the standards of the West Indies, they're a large and thriving business. Everything that was said in his lectures about his family's growth in fortune is true. His father, Joe or Joseph, founded the business. Neville talks frequently about his older brother Victor, in his lectures. I'm not going to go into all the details here because I have a more exciting example that I want to bring to you, but everything that Neville described about the rise of his family's fortune matches business records and reportage in West Indian newspapers.

Neville lived in Greenwich Village for many years. In the 1940s he was at 32 Washington Square on the west side of Washington Square Park. He spent many years happily there. Now, here was a story that interested me in his lectures and I determined to track down the truth of it. Neville was drafted into the Army on November 12, 1942, just a little less than a year into America's entry to World War II, so it was at the height of war. Everybody was being drafted. He was a little old to be drafted. He was 37 at that time, but you could still be drafted up to age 45. He tells this story in several of his lectures.

He didn't want to be in the Army. He wanted no part of the war. He wanted to return home to Greenwich Village. At that time, he was married. He had a small daughter, Victoria or Vicky. He had a son from an earlier marriage. He wanted to go back to lecturing. He was in basic training in Louisiana. He asked his commanding officer for a discharge and the commanding officer definitively refused.

So Neville said that every night he would lay down in his cot and imagine himself back home in Greenwich Village, walking around Washington Square Park, back with his wife and family. Every night he'd go to bed in this sensation.

Night after night, he did this for several weeks. And he said that finally, out of the clear blue, the commanding officer came to him and said, "Do you still want to be discharged?" Neville said, "Yes, I do." "You're being honorably discharged," the officer told him.

As I read this, I doubted it. Why would the United States want to discharge a perfectly healthy, athletic male at the height of the America's entry into the Second World War? It made no sense. I started looking for Neville's military records to see if there were other things that would back this up. Neville claimed that he entered the military in late 1942 and then he was honorably discharged about four months later using nothing other than these mental-emotive techniques.

I found Neville's surviving military records. He was, in fact, inducted into the Army on November 12, 1942. I spoke to an Army public affairs spokesman who confirmed that Neville was honorably discharged in March 1943, which is the final record of his U.S. Army pay statement. The reason for the discharge in military records is that he had to return to a "vital civilian occupation." I said to the spokesman, "This man was a metaphysical lecturer, that is not seen as a vital civilian occupation." And he said to me, "Well, unfortunately, the rest of Mr. Goddard's records were destroyed in a fire at a military records facility 1973"—one year following Neville's death.

I know that Neville was back in New York City because *The New Yorker* magazine ran surprisingly extensive profile of him in September of 1943, which places him back on the circuit. He was depicted speaking all around town—in midtown in the Actor's Church, in Greenwich Village, and he completely resumed his career, this "vital civilian occupation" as a metaphysical lecturer. Now, I can't tell you what happened. I can only tell you that the forensics as he described them were accurate. This was one of several instances in which he describes an unlikely story, claims that he used his method as I've described it them you, and, while I can't tell you exactly what happened, I can tell you that the forensics line up.

Neville filled out an application for naturalization and citizenship on September 1, 1943. His address was 32 Washington Square at the time, his age 38 years old. Everything he described in terms of his whereabouts added up.

THE SOURCE

I want to say a quick word about where this philosophy came from. Where did Neville get these ideas? His thought was wholly original but everyone has antecedents of some kind. Neville was part of a movement that I call "the positive-thinking movement." Positive-mind metaphysics was a very American philosophy, and it was very much a homegrown philosophy, but, at the same time, every thought that's ever been thought has been encountered by sensitive people in the search extending back to the mythical Hermes, who ancient people in West and Near East considered the progenitor of all ideas and all intellect.

Hermetic philosophy was a Greek-Egyptian philosophy that was written about and set down in the Greek language in the city of Alexandria a few decades following the death of Christ. Neville quotes from one of the Hermetic books in the lecture "Inner Conversations." A central Hermetic theme is that through proper preparation, diet, meditation, and prayer, the individual can be permeated by divine forces. This was a key tenet of Hermeticism. This outlook was reborn during the Renaissance when scholars and translators came to venerate the figure of Hermes Trismegistus, or thrice-greatest Hermes, a Greek term of veneration of Egypt's god of intellect Thoth. Hermes Trismegistus, a mythical man-god, was considered a great figure of antiquity by Renaissance thinkers, of a vintage as old as Moses or Abraham or older still.

Renaissance translators initially believed that the Hermetic literature—tracts that were signed by Hermes Trismegistus, whose name was adopted by Greek-Egyptian scribes—extended back to primeval antiquity. Hermetic writings were considered the source of earliest wisdom. This literature was later correctly dated to late antiquity. After the re-dating, Hermetic ideas eventually fell out of vogue. Some of the intellectual lights of the Renaissance had placed great hopes that the writings attributed to Hermes Trismegistus possessed great antiquity. And when those hopes of antiquity were and these writings were accurately dated to late antiquity, the readjustment of the timeline, I think tragically for Western civilization, convinced many people that the whole project of the Hermetic literature was somehow compromised. For that reason there are, to this day, relatively few quality translations of the Hermetic literature. The dating issue assumed too great a proportion in people's minds. The fact is, all ancient literature, just like all religions, are built from earlier ideas, and I believe the Hermetic philosophy was a retention of much older oral philosophy. Most scholars today agree with that.

In any case, the Hermetic ideas faded. Including the core principle that the human form could be permeated by something higher and could itself attain a kind of creative and clairvoyant power. These ideas that were so arousing, that created such hope and intrigue during Renaissance, got pushed to the margins. But they eventually reentered the public mind in part through the influence of Franz Anton Mesmer (1734–1815), who was a lawyer and a self-styled physician of Viennese descent. Mesmer appeared in Paris in 1778, in the decade preceding the French Revolution. He entered into royal courts with this radical theory that all of life was animated by this invisible etheric fluid which he called *animal magnetism.*

Mesmer maintained that if you place an individual into a kind of trance state, what we would call a hypnotic trance—recall Neville talking about this state of drowsiness, this hypnagogic state—you could then realign his or her animal magnetism, this ethereal life fluid, and cure physical or mental diseases, and, according to practitioners, introduce powers such as clairvoyance or the ability to speak in unknown foreign tongues. You could heal. You could empower. You could get at the life stuff of the individual. I was recently in a Walgreen's drugstore and saw an ad reading, "Mysterious and Mesmerizing," for a skin lotion. It's funny how occult language, unmoored from its meaning, lingers in daily life.

Mesmer was feted in royal courts but his philosophy aroused suspicion. At the instigation of King Louis XVI, Mesmerism was discredited by a royal commission in 1784. This investigatory commission was chaired by Benjamin Franklin, who at the time was America's ambassador to France. The commission concluded that there was no such thing as animal magnetism and that whatever cures or effects were experienced under the influence of a mesmeric trance were "in the imagination." But there the committee left dangling its most extraordinary question. If it's "in the imagination," why should there be any effects at all?

Mesmer's greatest students edged away from the idea of animal magnetism as some physical, ethereal fluid. They believed something else was at work. In their struggle for answers, they arrived at the first descriptions of what we would later call subliminal mind and then the subconscious or unconscious mind. Mesmer's proteges did not possess a psychological vocabulary—they preceded and in some regards prefigured modern psychology—but they knew that *something* was evident and effective in his theory of animal magnetism. The best students morphed the master's theories into an early, rough iteration of the subconscious mind. This is an overlooked and crucial basis for the growth of modern psychology. The terms subliminal and subconscious mind began to be heard in the 1890s.

Mesmer died in 1815. But his ideas were taken up in many quarters including, fatefully, by a New England clockmaker named Phineas Quimby (1802–1866). Starting in the late 1830s, Quimby began to experiment with how states of *personal excitement* could make him feel better physically. Quimby suffered from tuberculosis and he discovered that when he would take vigorous carriage rides in the Maine countryside, the effects of tuberculosis would lift. Quimby began to probe the state of his mood and the state of his physical wellbeing. He treated others and became known as a mental healer in the mid-1840s.

At first, Quimby worked with a teenaged boy named Lucius Burkmar. Lucius would enter a trance or hypnagogic state from which he was said to be able to clairvoyantly view people's bodily organs and diagnose and prescribe cures for diseases. Quimby discovered that sometimes the cures that Lucius prescribed, which were often botanical remedies or herbal teas, had previously been prescribed by physicians—and did not work. But when Lucius prescribed them, *they often did work*. The difference, Quimby concluded, was in the *confidence of the patient*. Quimby stopped working with Lucius and encouraged patients to arouse mental energies on their own.

American medicine in the mid-1840s was in a horrendously underdeveloped state. It was the one area of the sciences in which American lagged behind Europe. People had some reason to be driven to mental healers and prayer healers because, if anything, they were less dangerous than most of what was then standard allopathic medicine, which involved measures that were medieval. Physicians were performing bloodletting, administering mercury and other poisons and narcotics. At the very least, the mental healing movement caused no harm.

And, according to historical letters, articles, and diaries, sometimes it did a lot of good. Someone who briefly served as a student to Quimby was Mary Baker Eddy (1821–1910), who founded her own movement called Christian Science. Eddy taught that the healing ministry of Christ is an ever-present fact that is still going on on Earth, and that individuals could be healed by the realization that there is only one true reality and that is this great divine mind that created the universe and that animates everything around us; and further that matter, these forms that we live in, and the floorboards underneath our feet, are not real. They are illusory, as are illness, prejudice, violence, and all human corruption. Eddy taught that through prayer and proper understanding of Scripture, the individual could be healed. She was a remarkable figure. Sometimes people will say, in a far too hasty way, "Well, she took all her ideas from Quimby." It's not that simple. Her interlude with Quimby in the early 1860s was vitally important in her development; but her ideas were uniquely her own. She was an extraordinary figure. I don't think we've taken full measure in this culture of how influential Mary Baker Eddy's ideas have been.

Another figure who become indirectly influential in this healing movement was Emanuel Swedenborg (1688–1772), a Swedish scientist and mystic who worked primarily in the 1700s. Swedenborg's central idea was that the mind is a conduit, a capillary, of cosmic laws, and everything that occurs in the world, including our own thoughts, mirrors events in an invisible world, a spiritual world, which we do not see but always interact with. Everything that men and women do on Earth, Swedenborg taught, is a reflection of something occurring in this unseen world, and our minds are almost like receiving stations, spiritual telegraphs, for messages and ideas from a cosmic plane in which we cannot directly participate but are vitally linked.

Swedenborg was an influence on a Methodist minister named Warren Felt Evans, who was also a contemporary of Quimby's, and who briefly worked with him. Evans wrote a book in 1869 called *The Mental Cure* which was the first book to use the term "new age" in the spiritual sense that it's used today. Evans believed that through prayer, proper direction of thought, use of affirmations, and assumption of a confident mental state, the individual could be cured. *The Mental Cure* is not read anywhere today. Yet it is a surprisingly sprightly book. You'd be surprised. When I first had to read *The Mental Cure* I braced myself but I found that its pages turn quite effortlessly. Evans was a brilliant writer. All of his books are obscure today. But he was a seminal figure in the creation of a positive-thinking movement.

More indirectly, the British poet William Blake also had a certain influence on this movement, and on Neville in particular. Blake believed that humans dwell in this coarse world where we are imprisoned in a fortress of illusions; but the one true mind, the great creative imagination of God, can course through us. We can "cleanse the doors of perception." We can feel the coursing of this great mind within us.

These are some of the same ideas that resounded in Hermeticism. There wasn't a direct connection, necessarily. First of all, there weren't many translations of some of the Hermetic literature, which a man like Blake could likely draw upon. People from different epochs and eras often arrived at these parallel cosmic ideas themselves. When academic writers approach New Thought or the positive-thinking movement, they sometimes make the mistake of conflating it with the idealist philosophy of figures like Berkeley, Kant, Hegel, and later Schopenhauer and Nietzsche. The positive-thinking figures were not directly influenced by the idealists. Those figures and their phraseology are absent in early positive-mind writings. People sometimes make the mistake of not realizing that in a country like America, which was a very agricultural country throughout most of the 19th century, little of this material was directly available.

As an example, consider the Tao Te Ching. This great ancient Chinese work on ethics and philosophy wasn't even translated into English until 1838. In the mid-1840s, there existed four English-language copies in all of the United States. One was in the library at Harvard, one was in Ralph Waldo Emerson's library which he lent out, and two were in private hands. It wasn't like somebody like Phineas Quimby, the New England clockmaker, who was experimenting with moods and the body, could locate Taoist or Hermetic philosophy, or could even read translations of Hegel. Literacy aside, many of these things weren't accessible. It's a mistake to conclude that because one system of thought mirrors another, that the preceding system is necessarily the birth mother of the later one. In the rural environs of America, many of the positive-mind theorists were independently coming up with these ideas.

Moving into the 20th century, we encounter a figure who directly influenced Neville—French mind theorist Emile Coué (1857–1926). Coué was a largely self-trained hypnotherapist. He died in 1926, but shortly before he died, he made two lecture tours of the United States. Coué was hugely popular in the US and in England. He had a key theory, which rested on the principle that when you enter a sleepy drowsy state, the hypnagogic state, your mind is uniquely supple, suggestible, and powerful. Coué came up with a method to use in conjunction with this state. His system was so simple that critics mocked it. You've probably heard of it. Coué told people to gently repeat the mantra, "Day by day, in every way, I am getting better and better." He said you should lay in bed and recite this just as you're drifting off at night and again just as you're coming to in the morning. Whisper it twenty times to yourself. You could knot a piece of string twenty times and take that piece of string with you, keep it at your bedside, so you could count off your repetitions like a rosary.

Coué had many thousands of followers, but he also became a figure of ridicule because the critics said: "How could such a simple idea possibly do anything for anyone?" Of course, they would not try it. To their minds, it was prima facie nonsense. Such an attitude reminds me of the character of Dr. Zaius from *Planet of the Apes* insisting that flight is a physical impossibility. Thought in the absence of experience is the impoverishment of our intellectual culture. Certainty in the absence of personal experience precludes effort.

In addition to the uses of hypnagogia, another of Coué's ideas appeared in Neville's thought system. You can find the language from time to time in Neville's lectures and writing. That is, within human beings exist two forces: *will* and *imagination*. The *will* is intellectual self-determination. The *imagination* is the mental images and emotionally conditioned reactions that populate our psyches, particularly with regard to self-image. Coué said that when imagination and will are in conflict, *imagination always win*. Your emotional state always overcomes your intellect.

As an example, Coué said, place a wooden plank on the floor and ask an average person to walk across it. He or she will have no problem. But if you raise that same wooden plank twenty feet off the ground, in many cases the person will be petrified even though there's no difference in the physical demand. They are capable of walking across it. The risk of falling is minimal. *The change in condition alone creates an emotional state that makes them more nervous and hence accident prone.* Coué believed it necessary to cultivate new imaginative images of ourselves. We cannot do that through the intellect alone. But we can do so by making using of this very subtle hypnagogic state. He called his method autosuggestion. It was self-hypnosis essentially. Neville adopted the method, if not the same assumptions behind it.

THE MYSTIC IN LIFE

There are few pictures of Neville. His smiles glowingly in rare pictures toward the end of his life. He died young at age 67 in 1972. He died of heart failure in West Hollywood where he was living with his family. Until the end, his voice and his powers of communication never left him. They absolutely resonated.

It's interesting sometimes to look at the lives of mystical figures like Neville who are hard to pin down, but who did lead domestic lives. There was a little piece in the *Los Angeles Times* on October 21, 1962: "Ms. Goddard Named as College President." It went on, "Miss Victoria Goddard, daughter of Mr. and Mrs. Neville Goddard, has been appointed co-chairman of campus publicity by the student government president at Russell Sage College for New York. She is an English major." This was Neville's daughter.

Now, Victoria Goddard or Vicky as she's known, is still living. She lives in Los Angeles in the family house that she once resided in with her parents. She avoids publicity and contact with people who are interested in Neville's ideas. I've tried to reach out to her but she has no interest in being in touch. She did give her approval indirectly to an anthology of Neville's writings that I wrote an introduction to, but she doesn't want contact with his students. She wants to lead her own existence. But it's funny sometimes we come across little things like this article or a photograph and realize that every one of us share the same workaday concerns.

For all of Neville's wonderful mystical theories, I just have to share this little discourse that he went into about Liquid-Plumr in a lecture that he delivered in 1970. I found this a delightful reminder of how the ordinary steps into all of our lives even when we're trying to deal with cosmic and mystical concerns. He told an audience in 1970:

So you buy something because of highly publicized TV promotions. Someone highly publicized what is called "Liquid-Plumr." And so I had some moment in my bathroom where the sink was all stopped up, so I got the Liquid-Plumr. Poured it in, in abundance. It said it's heavier than water, and it would go all the way down and just eat up everything that is organic and will not hurt anything that is not organic, so I poured it in. Water still remained; it didn't go down. Called the plumber the next day. He couldn't come that day but he would come the next day. So it was forty-eight hours. So when he came the entire sink was eaten away by the Liquid-Plumr. So I asked him: "Does this thing work?" He said: "It does for two people: the one who manufactures it, and the one who sells it." They are the only ones who profit by the Liquid-Plumr. And so you turned on the TV and you saw it and you bought it. It is still on TV and I am sinning, because to sin by silence when I should protest makes cowards of us all. But I haven't protested to the station that advertises this nonsense and I haven't protested to the place where I got it or to anyone who manufactures it, so I am the silent sinner. Multiply me because of my embarrassment. Here is a sink completely eaten up by Liquid-Plumr.

"The silent sinner," he called himself. I lodge letters of protest and phone calls from time to time, so I can sympathize with everything Neville says here.

Neville published a variety of books during his lifetime, most of them quite short. There was a company in Los Angeles called G and J Publishing which issued most of his books. A symbol appeared on most of his covers, which he devised himself. It was a heart with an eye to symbolize eternal vision, inner vision, and it was part of a fruit-bearing tree. As the emotive state of man conceives, so the tree brings forth fruit.

In 1964, Neville published an extremely rare pamphlet called, *He Breaks The Shell*. On its cover you can see a little cherub or angelic figure coming out of a human head. Neville described this mystical experience and said that this is an experience that all of us will have either in this lifetime or another; and that the whole purpose of human existence is to be reborn from your imagination; and your imagination, as we experience it, is physically lodged in your skull, entombed in this kind of a womb. Christ was crucified in Golgotha, place of the skull. Neville believed that we each will be reborn from within our own skull, and that we will have an actual physical experience, maybe in the form of a dream, but a vivid, tactile experience of being reborn from out of the base of our skull. We will know, in that moment, that we are fulfilling our essential purpose.

He described this quite vividly. He had this experience in New York City in 1959 where he had an enormously tactile, sensationally real dream of being reborn from out of the skull. Minerva was said to have been reborn from the skull of Zeus or Jupiter. Christ was crucified at the place of the skull. "You and I," Neville said, "will be reborn from within our skull." In the late 1960s a booking agent told him, "Listen, you've got to stop telling this story at your talks. It's freaking everyone out. People want to hear the get-rich stuff." He told Neville that he if did not change course he'd have no audience left. "Then I'll tell it to the bare walls," Neville replied. He spoke of his mystical experience for the rest of his career until he died in 1972.

I reissued one of Neville's books recently, *The Power of Awareness*. I felt that, for the first time, Neville's books needed to be packaged in a way that fits their dignity, and this is a beautiful edition that I took great joy in working on because I thought it represented him with the right degree of dignity.

I want to quote from Neville's voice. He spoke in such beautiful, resonant language, so unhaltingly, never a pause, never an uncertainty. He knew his outlook so well, he could share it effortlessly. Here is his voice.

> So I'm telling you of the power within you and that power is your own wonderful human imagination. And that is the only God in the world. There is no other God. That is the Jesus Christ of Scripture, so tonight take it seriously. If you really have an objective in this world and you're waiting for something to happen on the outside to make it so, forget it. Do it in your own wonderful human imagination. Actually bring it into being in your own imagination. Conjure a scene which would imply the fulfillment of that dream and lose yourself in

the action as you contemplate it, and completely lose yourself in that state. If you're completely absorbed in it, you will objectify it and you will see it seemingly independent of your perception of it. But even if you do not have that intensity, if you lose yourself in it and feel it to true—the imaginal act—then drop it. In a way you do not know, it will become true.

If you are interested in hearing more of Neville, you can go online and find lectures that are posted on YouTube and almost everywhere. He allowed people who came to presentations to tape record them and freely distribute them. He claimed copyright over nothing, and that, to me, is the mark of a real leader. That's the mark of a real thinker. You don't have to join anything. You don't have to ask anybody permission for anything. You don't have to pay any dues. You don't have to buy anything. You just start.

NEVILLE'S CIRCLE

I want to say a quick word about some of the people who have been influenced by Neville today. One of them is the major-league baseball pitcher, Barry Zito, who actually introduced me to Neville. I was doing an article about Barry in 2003 and he said to me, "Oh, you must be into

Neville," and I said, "I've never heard of him." He said, "Really? You never heard of him?" He was the first one who got me interested in Neville's thought, and that was a huge influence in my life. It was almost 10 years ago to this very day and in many regards put me where I am today.

The New Age writer Wayne Dyer wrote a lot about Neville in his most recent book which is called *Wishes Fulfilled*. But a really remarkable influence that Neville brought into the world came in the form his subtle impact on the writer, Carlos Castaneda, of whom I'm a great admirer. I want to read a short passage from my forthcoming book, *One Simple Idea*:

> By the mid-1950s, Neville's life story exerted a powerful pull on a budding writer whose own memoirs of mystic discovery later made him a near-household name: Carlos Castaneda. Castaneda told his own tales of tutelage under a mysterious instructor, in his case a Native American sorcerer named Don Juan. Castaneda first discovered Neville through an early love interest in Los Angeles, Margaret Runyan, who was among Neville's most dedicated students. A cousin of American storyteller Damon Runyon, Margaret wooed the stocky Latin art student at a friend's house, slipping Carlos a slender Neville volume called *The*

Search, in which she had inscribed her name and phone number. The two became lovers and later husband and wife. Runyan spoke frequently to Castaneda about her mystical teacher Neville, but he responded with little more than mild interest— with one exception.

In her memoirs, Runyan recalled Castaneda growing fascinated when the conversation turned to Neville's discipleship under an exotic teacher. She wrote:

> It was more than the message that attracted Carlos, it was Neville himself. He was so mysterious. Nobody was really sure who he was or where he had come from. There were vague references to Barbados in the West Indies and his being the son of an ultra-rich plantation family, but nobody knew for sure. They couldn't even be sure about this Abdullah business, his Indian teacher, who was always way back there in the jungle, or someplace. The only thing you really knew was that Neville was here and that he might be back next week, but then again . . .

"There was," Runyon concluded, "a certain power in that position, an appealing kind of freedom in the lack of past and Carlos knew it."

Carlos knew it. Both Neville and Castaneda were dealing the same basic idea, and one that has a certain pedigree in America's alternative spiritual culture: tutelage under hidden spiritual masters.

Neville again and again told this story, that there was a turbaned black man of Jewish descent who tutored him starting in 1931 in kabbalah, Scripture, number symbolism, and mental metaphysics. He described Abdullah as this somewhat taciturn, mysterious figure who he met one day at a metaphysical lecture in 1931. Neville walked in and Abdullah said to him, "Neville, you're six months late." Neville said, "I had never seen this man before." Abdullah continued, "The brothers told me you were coming and you're six months late." He said they spent the next five years together studying.

Neville had his first true awakening experience in the winter of 1933. He was dying to get out of the Manhattan winter. He wanted to spend Christmas back home with his family in Barbados. He had no money and Abdullah said to him, "Walk the streets of Manhattan as if you are there and you shall be." And so Neville said he would walk the gray wintry streets of the Upper West Side with the feeling that he was in the palm-lined lanes of Barbados. He would go to see Abdullah, telling him, "It isn't working. I'm still here." And Abdullah would slam the door in his face and say, "You're not here. You're in Barbados."

Then one day, before the last ship departed for Barbados, his brother, Victor, from out of the blue, without any physical intercession on Neville's part, sent him a first-class steamer ticket and $50. "Come spend winter with us in Barbados," he wrote. Neville said he was transformed by the experience. He felt that it was Abdullah's law of mental assumption came to his rescue.

Now, this idea of mysterious spiritual masters got popularized in modern Western culture through the influence of Madame Blavatsky and her partner Colonel Henry Steel Olcott who founded the movement of Theosophy in New York City in 1975. They claimed to be under the tutelage of hidden spiritual masters, Master Koot Hoomi, who was said to be Tibetan, and Master Morya who was said to be Indian. These adepts, they said, would send them phenomenally produced letters, advising them what to do, giving them directions, giving them advice, giving them succor. Around that time, Colonel Olcott and Madame Blavatsky were living in a building which is still standing at the corner of 8th Avenue of West 47th Street which was known as the Lamasery, their headquarters or salon, where they dwelt on the second floor. Today it is an Econo Lodge. None of the people who worked there were very entranced with my attempts to explain the history of the building.

Colonel Olcott said that one time in the winter of 1877, Master Morya materialized in his room and directed him and Madame Blavatsky to relocate to the nation of India, which they did the following year. They helped instigate the Indian independence movement. Olcott went on speaking tours all over the Near East, Far East, Japan, Sri Lanka. He helped instigate a rebirth of Buddhism throughout the East. Blavatsky and Olcott were enormously effective in their way. Colonel Olcott attributed all of it to the presence of these mysterious spiritual masters, these great turbaned figures somewhere from the East who had given them instruction.

Now, I first wrote about Neville in an article that was published in February 2005 in *Science of Mind* magazine called "Searching for Neville Goddard." Things had been fairly quiet around Neville for many years, and that article attracted a lot of interest. I started receiving phone calls and e-mail after e-mail asking me, who was Abdullah? Did he exist? Could he be identified? I would tell people at the time that I thought Abdullah was a kind of a mythos that Neville might have borrowed, clipped and pasted, from Theosophy. I didn't think there was any evidence to show that Abdullah was a real person, and I thought the dramatic claims around him were probably Neville's mythmaking.

Now, to my surprise, I discovered something about Abdullah through another figure in the positive thinking movement, a man named Joseph Murphy, who died in

1981, and who wrote a very popular book, which some of you may have read, called *The Power of Your Subconscious Mind*. Shortly before his death, Murphy gave a series of interviews to a French-speaking minister from Quebec. The interviewer published his book only in French with Quebec press. It is called *Dialogues with Joseph Murphy* and in these interviews Murphy offhandedly remarks that he, too, was a student of Abdullah. Murphy actually came to New York around the same time as Neville in 1922. He migrated from Ireland. Murphy worked as a pharmacist at the Algonquin Hotel. They used to have a little pharmacy in their lobby. And Murphy also became a metaphysical lecturer and was acquainted with Neville for several years. He stated very simply and matter-of-factly that Abdullah was his teacher too, and that he was a very real man.

I began to look around and correspond with people, and I came to feel, over the past few years, that I happened upon a figure who might actually be Abdullah. He was Arnold Josiah Ford. Ford was a mystic, black nationalist, and part of a movement called the Black Hebrew Movement which still exists in various forms. Ford was born in Barbados, Neville's home island, in 1877. Ford emigrated to Harlem in 1910. He became involved with Marcus Garvey's Universal Negro Improvement Association, of which he was musical director. In surviving photographs Ford, like Abdullah, is turbaned.

In addition to being a dedicated follower of Marcus Garvey—who had his own mind-power metaphysics, about which I'll say a quick word in a moment—Ford was also part of a movement called Ethiopianism. It was a precursor to Rastafarianism. Ford believed, as the Rastafarian people do, as many other people do with good reason, that Ethiopia, one of the oldest continuous civilizations on Earth and one of the most populous nations in Africa, was home to a lost tribe of Israel, which, in this line of teaching, had its own blend of what we know as traditional historical Judaism and mystical teachings and mental metaphysics.

The movement of Ethiopianism believed that this lost African-Israelite tribe harbored a great wealth of ancient teachings that had been lost to most modern people. The Ethiopianism movement believed in mind-power metaphysics and mental healing. Ford was considered a rabbi and he had his own African-American congregation in Harlem. He described himself a man of authentic Israelite and Jewish descent. Writing in 1946, occult philosopher Israel Regardie described Neville's Abdullah as an "Ethiopian rabbi." Regardie, who had been a secretary to the occultist, Aleister Crowley, is quoted on Neville in the introduction.

According to census records, Ford was living in Harlem 1931. He identified his occupation to the census taker as rabbi. That was the same year that Neville met

Abdullah. (Although he later gave Abdullah's address as the Upper West Side, not Harlem.) Neville may have been playing around with the name a little bit. He would affectionately refer to Abdullah in his lectures as *Ab*. Ab is a variant of the Hebrew word *abba* for father. Perhaps he saw Abdullah, Ford, as kind of a father figure. He said they studied metaphysics, Scripture, Kabbalah together for five years. Ford has been written about in histories of the Black Hebrew Movement as a key figure who brought authentic knowledge of the Hebrew language, Talmud, and Kabbalah into the Black Hebrew Movement as it existed in Harlem at that time.

Ford was a person of some learning. He was, as I said, a follower of Marcus Garvey, a figure about whom I write in *Occult America*. Garvey has not been properly understood in our culture. He was a pioneering black nationalist figure. He was a great pioneering activist and voice of liberation. He was also very much into his own brand of mental metaphysics. You might recognize this statement of Garvey's which Bob Marley adapted in the lyrics to *Redemption Song:* "We are going to emancipate ourselves from mental slavery because whilst others might free the body, none but ourselves can free the mind." Garvey's speeches are shot through with New Thought language, with the language of mental metaphysics. This was an essential part of Garvey's outlook. This perspective was also essential to the culture of Ethiopianism, which saw Ethiopia's crowned emperor, Haile Selassie, who was coronated in 1930, as a messianic figure. The movement of Ethiopianism morphed into Rastafarianism. It started in the mid-1930s.

Now, there are a lot of correspondences between Arnold Josiah Ford and Neville's description of Abdullah, including physical correspondences, the turban and such. But for all that I've noted, the timeline does not match up sufficiently to make any of this conclusive; because Ford left America sometime in 1931, and he moved to the Ethiopian countryside. After Haile Selassie was coronated as emperor, he offered a land grant to any African-American willing to emigrate to Ethiopia. The emperor saw Ethiopia in a way that matched Ford's ideals as a kind of African-Israel. Haile Selassie wanted Afro-Caribbean and Afro-American people to move, or to come home as he saw it, to Ethiopia, so he offered land grants.

Ford and about thirty followers of Ethiopianism in New York accepted the land grants. There's been some debate about when Ford left, but I have a *New York Times* article that places Ford in New York City still in December 1930. He didn't leave until 1931. That was the same year that Neville said they met. The timeline doesn't match up because Neville said they studied together for five years, so it's possible that Ford was one of several teachers that

Neville had, and he created a kind of composite figure who he called Abdullah, Ab, father, of whom Ford may have been a part.

Now, in a coda to Ford's life, I must take note that it was a tougher and braver and more brutal existence back then in some regards. Ford, who for 20 years has been living as a musician and a rabbi in Harlem, moved to rural Ethiopia, the northern part of this nation, to accept Haile Selassie's land grant. He died there in 1935. Tragically, there are no records of Ford's life in Ethiopia. It must have been very difficult. Imagine being a metropolitan person and uprooting yourself to a completely rural setting in a developing nation in the 1930s, and Mussolini is beating the war drum, and Mussolini's fascist troops invaded Ethiopia just weeks after Ford's death, across the north border. This was a man who put himself through tremendous ordeals for his principles. I cannot conclude that Ford was Abdullah. But Murphy's testimony suggests that there *was* an Abdullah, and I think Ford corresponds in many ways—and I write about this in *One Simple Idea*; there probably is some intersection there.

There's another figure I want to mention of a very different kind whose thought had some indirect intersection with Neville's, and that is Aleister Crowley, the British occultist. Crowley made a very interesting statement in a

book that he received in a way that we might call chan-
neled perception in 1904; it was later published broadly
in 1938 called *The Book of the Law*. In his introduction,
Crowley writes:

> Each of us has thus an universe of his own, but
> it is the same universe for each one as soon as it
> includes all possible experience. This implies the
> extension of consciousness to include all other
> consciousnesses. In our present stage, the object
> that you see is never the same as the one that I see;
> we infer that it is the same because your experi-
> ence tallies with mine on so many points that the
> actual differences of our observation are negligi-
> ble . . . Yet all the time neither of us can know any-
> thing . . . at all beyond the total impression made
> on our respective minds.

Neville said something similar:

> Do you realize that no two people live in the same
> world? We may be together now in this room, but
> we will go home tonight and close our doors on
> entirely different worlds. Tomorrow, we will go to
> work where we'll meet others but each one of us
> lives in our own mental and physical world.

Neville meant this in the most literal sense. He believed that every individual, possessed of his or her own imagination, is God, and that everyone you see, including me standing in this room, is rooted in you, as you are ultimately rooted in God.

You exist in this world of infinite possibilities and realities, and that, in fact, when you mentally picture something, you're not creating it—it already exists. You're claiming it. The very fact of being able to experience it mentally confirms that in this world of infinite possibilities, where imagination is the ultimate creative agent, everything that you can picture *already is*.

MIND SCIENCE

Some of the things that Neville said prefigured studies both in psychical research and quantum physics. I want to say a quick word about that. One of my heroes is, J.B. Rhine, a psychical researcher who performed tens of thousands of trials at Duke University in the 1930s and beyond to test for clairvoyant perception. Rhine often used a five-suit deck of cards called Zener cards; if you were guessing a card, you had a one-in-five chance, 20 percent, of naming the right card. As Rhine documented in literally tens of thousands of trials, with meticulous clinical control, certain individuals persistently, under controlled conditions, scored higher than a chance hit of 20 percent.

It wasn't always dramatically higher. It wasn't like Zeus was aiming lightning bolts at the Earth. But if someone over the course of thousands of trials keeps scoring 25 percent, 26 percent, 27 percent, beyond all chance possibility, and the results are parsed, juried, gone over, reviewed, you have some anomalous transfer of information going on in a laboratory setting. Rhine's research was real. And Rhine noticed—and he had this quietly monumental way of describing things, he would make some observation in a footnote that could be extraordinary—that the correlation to a high success rate of hits on the Zener cards was usually a feeling of enthusiasm, positive expectation, hopefulness, belief in the possibility of ESP, and an encouraging environment. Then when boredom or physical exhaustion would set in, or interest would wane, the results would go down. If interest was somehow renewed, revised, if there was a feeling of comity in the testing room, the results would go up.

We as a culture haven't begun to deal with the implications of Rhine's experiments. There was another parapsychologist, Charles Honorton, who began a series of experiments in 1970s—I see him as Rhine's successor—called the *ganzfeld* experiments. Ganzfeld is German for whole field. Honorton experimented on subjects who were in a hypnagogic state, the state of drowsiness. Honorton and his collaborators theorized that if you could induce the near-sleep state in an individual, put somebody in conditions of comfortable isolation, fit them with eye coverings and headphones emitting white noise or some kind of negative sound to listen to, put them in a greatly relaxed state, it might be possible to heighten the appearance of some kind of clairvoyant faculty.

His test was to place a subject, a receiver, into a comfortable isolation tank, and to place another subject, a sender, in a different room. Then the sender attempted to mentally convey an image—such as a flower, a rocket, a boat, or something else—to the receiver, and see what happens. These tests generally used four images. Three were decoys, one was actual. Again, in certain subjects, and also in the subjects as a whole in the form of meta-analysis, Honorton found over and over again results that showed a higher than 25 percent chance hit when subjects were placed into the hypnagogic state.

We're in this state all the time. When you're napping, when you're dozing off at your desk, when you're going to sleep at night, when you're waking up in the morning. Neville's message is: *use it*. Honorton died very young in 1992 at age 46. He had suffered health problems his whole life. If he had lived, his name would, I believe, be as well-known as J.B. Rhine. He was a great parapsychologist.

There's another field burgeoning today called neuroplasticity that relates to some of Neville's sights. In short, brain imaging shows that repeat thoughts change the pathways through which electrical impulses travel in your brain. This has been used to treat obsessive compulsive disorder. A research psychologist named Jeffery Schwartz at UCLA has devised a program that ameliorates and dissipates obsessive thoughts. Schwartz's program teaches patients and people in his clinical trials to substitute something in place of an obsessive thought at the very moment they experience it. This diversion may be a pleasurable physical activity, listening to music, jogging, whatever they want, just anything that gets them off that obsessive thought. Schwartz has found through brain imaging, and many scientists have replicated this data, that if you repeat an exercise like that, eventually biologic changes manifest in the brain, neuropathways change, thoughts themselves alter brain biology as far as electrical impulses are concerned.

A New Thought writer in 1911, who theorized without any of the contemporary brain imaging and neuroscience, came up with exactly the same prescription. His name was John Henry Randall. Randall called it *substitution*. His language and the language used today by 21st century researchers in neuroplasticity is extraordinarily similar.

Finally, we have emerging from the field of quantum physics an extraordinary set of questions, which have been coming at us actually for 80-plus years, about the extent to which observation influences the manifestation of subatomic particles. I want to give a very brief example. Basically, quantum physics experiments have shown that if you direct a wave of particles, often in the form of a light wave, at a target system, perhaps a double-slit box or two boxes, the wave of light will collapse into a particle state, it will go from a wave state to a particle state. This occurs when a conscious observer is present or a measurement is occurring. Interference patterns demonstrate that the particle-like properties of wave of light *at one time appeared in both boxes*. Only when someone decided to look or to take a measurement did the particles become localized in one box.

In 1935, physicist Erwin Schrodinger noted that the conclusions of these quantum experiments were so outrageous, were so contrary to all observed experience, that he devised a thought experiment called Schrodinger's Cat in order to highlight this surreality. Schrodinger did not intend his thought experiment to endorse quantum theorizing. He intended it to compel quantum theorists to deal with the ultimate and, what he considered, absurdist conclusions of their theories—theories which have never been overturned, theories which have been affirmed for 80 years. Now, Schrodinger's Cat comes down to this, it can be put this way: You take two boxes. You put a cat into one of the two boxes. You direct a subatomic particle at the boxes. One box is empty, one box holds the cat. Inside the box with the cat is what he called a "diabolical device." This diabolical device trips a beaker of poison when it comes in contact with a subatomic particle, thus killing the cat.

So, you do your experiment. You direct the particle and you go to check the boxes. Which box is the particle in? Is the cat dead? Is the cat alive? The cat is *both*, Schrodinger insisted. It must be *both* because the subatomic particle can be shown to exist in more than one place, in a wave state, until someone checks, and thus localizes it into a particle state, occupying one place. Hence, you must allow for both outcomes—you have a dead/alive cat. That makes no sense. All of lived experience says that you've got two boxes; you've got one cat; the cat's dead if you fired into the box with the cat; or the cat's alive if you fired into the other box. Schrodinger said, "Not so." Interference experiments demonstrate that at one point the subatomic particle was in a *wave state*; it was non-local; it existed only in potential; it existed in both boxes and, given the nature of quantum observation, potentially everywhere. It is only when you go to check and open one of the boxes that the particle becomes localized. *It was in both boxes until a conscious observer made the decision to check.*

A later group of physicists argued there's no doubting Schrodinger's conclusion, and in fact, if you were to check eight hours later, you would not only find a cat that was living/dead, but you would find a living cat that was hungry because it hadn't been fed for eight hours. The timing itself created a past, present, and future for the cat—a reality selected out of infinite possibilities. Schrodinger didn't intend for his thought experiment to affirm this radical departure from reality. He intended it to expose what he considered the absurdist conclusions of quantum physics. But quantum physics data kept mounting and mounting, and Schrodinger's thought experiment became to some physicists a very real illustration of the extraordinary physical impossibilities that we were seeing in the world of quantum physics.

The implication is that we live in a serial universe—that there are infinite realities, whether we experience them or not; and our experience of one of these realties rests on observation. If we can extrapolate from the extraordinary behaviors of subatomic particles, it stands to reason that parallel events and potentials are all are occurring simultaneously. Why don't we experience any of this? Our world is seemingly controlled by Newtonian mechanics. There aren't dead/alive cats. There are singular events. Why don't we experience quantum reality?

Today, a theory that makes the rounds among quantum physicists that when something gets bigger and bigger—remember these experiments are done on subatomic particles, the smallest isolated fragments of matter—when we pull back from a microscopic view of things, we experience what is known as "information leakage." The world gets less and less clear as it gets bigger; as we exit the subatomic level and enter the mechanical level that is familiar, we lose information about what's really going on.

American philosopher William James made the same observation in 1902. James said that when you view an object under a microscope, you're getting so much information; but more and more of that information is lost as you pan back. This is true of all human experience. A cohort of quantum physicists today says the same thing: that the actions of the particle lab are occurring around us always, but we don't know it because we lose information in this coarse physical world that we live in.

Neville said something similar. He said that you radiate the world around you by the persuasiveness of your imagination and feelings. A quantum physicist might call this observation. But in our three-dimensional world, Neville said, time beats so slowly that we do not always observe the relationship between the visible world and our inner nature. You and I can contemplate a desire and become it, but because of the slowness of time, it is easy to forget what we formerly set out to worship or destroy. Quantum physicists speak of "information leakage;" Neville basically spoke of "time leakage." Time moves so slowly for us that we lose the sense of cause and effect.

"Scientists will one day explain why there is a serial universe," Neville said in 1948, "but in practice, how you use the serial universe to change the future is more important."

TRY

I want to leave you with a slogan of an American occultist P.B. Randolph who lived in New York City. He was a man of African-American descent and a tremendously original thinker and mystical experimenter. He died at the young age of 49 in 1875. This was his personal slogan: *TRY*. That's all. *TRY*. This slogan later appeared in letters signed by the spiritual masters Koot Hoomi and Morya, which started reaching Colonel Henry Steel Olcott in 1870s. The first appeared about two months before Randolph's death. The letters used the same slogan: *TRY*.

What you're hearing now is something to try. Neville's challenge was as ultimate as it was simple: "Put my ideas to the test." Prove them to yourself or dismiss them, but what a tragedy would be not to try. It's all so simple.

I want to conclude with words from William Blake, who was one of Neville's key inspirations later in life. Blake described the coarsened world of the senses that we live in. He described such things sometimes in matters of geography. When he would say England, he didn't mean England the nation exactly. He meant the coarse world in which men and women find themselves, the world in which we see so little, and the parameters close in so tightly that we don't know what's really going on. Then the poet would talk about Jerusalem, which he saw as a greater world, as a reality, created through the divine imagination, which runs through all men and women.

I want to close with William Blake's ode "Jerusalem" from 1810. I hope you'll try to hear these words as Neville himself heard them.

And did those feet in ancient time
Walk upon Englands mountains green:
And was the holy Lamb of God,
On Englands pleasant pastures seen!

And did the Countenance Divine,
Shine forth upon our clouded hills?
And was Jerusalem builded here,
Among these dark Satanic Mills?

Bring me my Bow of burning gold:
Bring me my arrows of desire:
Bring me my Spear: O clouds unfold!
Bring me my Chariot of fire!

I will not cease from Mental Fight,

Nor shall my sword sleep in my hand:

Till we have built Jerusalem,

In Englands green & pleasant Land.

QUESTIONS AND ANSWERS

If there are a few questions, I'd be happy to take them.

Speaker: Can you do multiple wishes, say if there are three that you wish?

Mitch: Neville's own students in his lifetime asked him that very thing, and I'm in the same place myself because it's hard sometimes to limit one's wishes to one thing. Neville felt it was more effective if you limit it to one thing at a time; but he said that this was by no means a limit, you didn't have to limit yourself. The key thing is to feel the desire intensely and to hold your mental emotive picture with clarity and simplicity, and to stick with it. He did say he felt that at the time interval would be lessened if you limit yourself to one thing at a time. That was his practice, but he did not call it a must.

Speaker: I wanted something that didn't last, so to try to achieve that, do I meditate on it? How do I get result?

Mitch: Neville's idea was to enact a scene that would naturally transpire when the desired thing comes to pass. There may be many events that would transpire if that thing came to pass, but he said to select just one that has a particular emotional resonance, and then see yourself doing it over and over. Something as simple as a handshake or climbing a ladder. Just take one that has act emotional gravity and be persistent.

Speaker: Do you think that given his predilection for inner vision that there's any evidence suggest that Abdullah may have been a channel? Abdullah may have been a channel or a channel within Neville?

Mitch: Oh, that's an interesting question. He always referred to Abdullah as a flesh-and-blood figure, and he said Abdullah lived in an apartment on West 72nd Street, which I've visited, and he would talk about Abdullah in very physical, vivid terms, so he certainly described him as a flesh-and-blood being.

Speaker: You described many of the techniques, including the technique of walking in a cold winter day to get the feeling of being in another place. This is just other technique for the astral body. Basically, what he's describing is the emotional astral body being developed, of which one expression would be manifesting that state here, but it sounds like he could easily develop another technique because this sounds very limited.

Mitch: He does represent techniques such as walking and imagining himself in the palm tree-lined lanes in Barbados; but he most often came back to this idea of physical immobility and the uses of a hypnagogic state, that drowsy state. He again and again said that others can experiment, and should experiment, but that he personally found that to be the simplest and the most effective method. He would say sometimes he would enter the hypnagogic state and just feel thankful or try to seize upon one expression like *it is wonderful*. He might do that if he didn't have a specific thing that he was longing for at that moment. So he did experiment with some other techniques and points of view. He did said one lecture, "You praise others and you will shine," because it was very important to try to use these techniques to the benefit of another person. For example, if you have a friend who's looking for a job, you might form the mental picture of congratulating him or her on finding the perfect job because Neville believed in the oneness of humanity in the absolute most literal sense. There was no sentimentality about it. He felt that every individual was God.

Speaker: Did he say that he believed that the universe is holographic?

Mitch: He would say, and again, he sometimes made statements more in passing than full on, but he would say explicitly that we live in a universe of infinite possibilities, and everything that you desire, by the very fact of desiring it, because your imagination is a creative agent, already exists. It is a question of just claiming it, which is why it's so important to think from the desire fulfilled. It doesn't matter if you open your eyes or your checkbook or anything else and, of course, reality as we presently know it comes rushing back in. You must continue to think from the wish fulfilled, which he said was tantamount to selecting a reality that already existed. Schrodinger said there's a dead/alive cat. Neville would have said there are infinite outcomes and they all exist.

Speaker: Regarding the slowness of time, I'm curious what his thoughts were as far as the timetables for his technique.

Mitch: He said that we experience definite time intervals and that a time interval is part of the nature of our existence. I may want a new house and I may want that house right now, and I may think from the end of having that house, but he said, in effect, "The fact of the world that we experience here and now is that the trees have to grow to produce wood. The wood has to be harvested and the carpenter has to cut it. There will be time intervals." And he would say, "Your time interval could be an hour, it could be a month, it could be weeks, it could be years." There is a time interval. You nonetheless must stick to the ideal and try to make it just exquisitely effortless. He didn't endorse using the will. This isn't about saying, "I'm going to think this way." It is going into this meditative or drowsy or hypnagogic state, picturing something that confirms the realization of your desire, and feeling it emotionally; he said that when the method fails maybe it's because you're trying too hard. Neville wanted people to understand that there is an exquisite ease that one should feel with exercises.

Speaker: It sounds like he's saying that an emphasis on pure will would upset that balance.

Mitch: Yes. He used the word receptivity and he used the term time interval.

Speaker: Did Neville ever include other ideas outside of his system?

Mitch: He made very few references to other thought systems. He would frequently quote Scripture, mostly the New Testament. He felt the New Testament was a great blueprint and metaphor for human development in the figure of Christ. He felt that the Old Testament was

suggestive of the promise and the New Testament was fulfilling of the promise, and beyond that he made little reference to other thought systems. He was chiefly interested
in Scripture. He would talk about numbers; he loved symbolism. In his book *Your Faith Is Your Fortune* he talked
about certain aspects of the zodiac, astrology, and number
symbolism; but as time passed, he made fewer references
to other systems. Every now and again he'd use a piece
of language where I'll detect Emile Coué echoed; but so
much of what we talked about really came from his own
description of the world through his own experience. He
made little reference to other systems.

Speaker: I started reading your book *Occult America* and
there was a question in my mind—you write that a lot of
positive thinkers and people in New Age in American history have, on the one hand, kind of advocated basic techniques and methods for selfish success and money, and, on
the other hand, a lot of the better writers in New Age and
New Thought were passionately involved with and concerned about social movements. Where did Neville fall in
that dichotomy?

Mitch: That's a wonderful question and that was an aspect
for me that made it difficult to first enter Neville's work,
because he had no social concerns in the conventional

sense, and if people raised social concerns, he would push them aside and would insist that the world you see, whether it is of beauty or violence, is self-created. Prove the theory to yourself and then use the theory as you wish. You want to eliminate suffering? Eliminate suffering. But he ardently rejected fealty to any kind of social movement or ideal. He believed that coming into one's awareness of the godlike nature of imagination, of the literal God presence of the imagination, of having the experience of being reborn through one's skull, was the essential human task.

Speaker: As you said in your own book, a lot the 19th century Spiritualists were involved in movements like suffragism and abolitionism.

Mitch: Yes. Well, you know, these radical movements, radical political movements and radical spiritual movements, avant-garde politics, avant-garde spirituality, they all intersect. We often fail to understand how a figure like Marcus Garvey, for example, was involved with mental metaphysics; but as you get closer to the real lives of these people, the connection becomes more natural because they craved a new social order both spiritually and socially.

A Neville Goddard Timeline

1905: Neville Lancelot Goddard is born on February 19 to a British family in St. Michael, Barbados, the fourth child in a family of nine boys and one girl.

1922: At age seventeen Neville relocates to New York City to study theater. He makes a career as an actor and dancer on stage and silent screen, landing roles on Broadway, silent film, and touring Europe as part of a dance troupe.

1923: Neville briefly marries Mildred Mary Hughes, with whom he has a son, Joseph Goddard, born the following year.

1929: Neville marked this as the year that begin his mystical journey: "Early in the morning, maybe about three-thirty or four o'clock, I was taken in spirit into the Divine Council where the gods hold converse." (lecture from *Immortal Man*, 1977)

1931: After several years of occult study, Neville meets his teacher Abdullah, a turbaned black man of Jewish descent. The pair work together for five years in New York City.

1938: Neville begins his own teaching and speaking.

1939: Neville's first book, *At Your Command*, is published.

1940–1941: Neville meets Catherine Willa Van Schumus, who is to become his second wife.

1941: Neville publishes his longer and more ambitious book, *Your Faith Is Your Fortune*.

1942: Neville marries Catherine, who later that year gives birth to their daughter Victoria. Also that year, Neville publishes *Freedom for All: A Practical Application of the Bible*.

1942–1943: From November to March, Neville serves in the military before returning home to Greenwich Village in New York City. In 1943, Neville is profiled in *The New Yorker*.

1944: Neville publishes *Feeling Is the Secret*.

1945: Neville publishes *Prayer: The Art of Believing.*

1946: Neville meets mystical philosopher Israel Regardie in New York, who profiles him in his book *The Romance of Metaphysics*. Neville also publishes his pamphlet *The Search.*

1948: Neville delivers his classic "Five Lessons" lectures in Los Angeles, which many students find the clearest and most compelling summation of his methodology. It appears posthumously as a book.

1949: Neville publishes *Out of This World: Thinking Fourth Dimensionally.*

1952: Neville publishes *The Power of Awareness.*

1954: Neville publishes *Awakened Imagination.*

1955: Neville hosts radio and television shows in Los Angeles.

1956: Neville publishes *Seedtime and Harvest: A Mystical View of the Scriptures.*

1959: Neville undergoes the mystical experience of being reborn from his own skull. Other mystical experiences follow into the following year.

1960: Neville releases a spoken-word album.

1961: Neville publishes *The Law and Promise*; the final chapter, "The Promise," details the mystical experience he underwent in 1959, and others that followed.

1964: Neville publishes the pamphlet *He Breaks the Shell: A Lesson in Scripture*.

1966: Neville publishes his last full-length book, *Resurrection*, composed of four works from the 1940s and the contemporaneous closing title essay, which outlines the fullness of his mystical vision and of humanity's realization of its deific nature.

1972: Neville dies in West Hollywood at age 67 on October 1, 1972 from an "apparent heart attack" reports the *Los Angeles Times*. He is buried at the family plot in St. Michael, Barbados.

About the Authors

NEVILLE GODDARD was one of the most remarkable mystical thinkers of the past century. In more than ten books and thousands of lectures, Neville, under his solitary first name, expanded on one core principle: *the human imagination is God.* As such, he taught, everything that you experience results from your thoughts and feeling states. Born to an Anglican family in Barbados in 1905, Neville travelled to New York City at age seventeen in 1922 to study theater. Although he won roles on Broadway, in silent films, and toured internationally with a dance troupe, Neville abandoned acting in the early 1930s to dedicate himself to metaphysical studies and embark a new career as a writer and lecturer. He was a compelling presence at metaphysical churches, spiritual centers, and auditoriums until his death in West Hollywood, California, in 1972. Neville was not widely known during his lifetime, but today his books and lectures have attained new popularity. Neville's principles about the creative properties of the mind prefigured some of today's most radical quantum theorizing, and have influenced several major spiritual writers, including Carlos Castaneda and Joseph Murphy.

Mitch Horowitz is a PEN Award-winning historian whose books include *Occult America, One Simple Idea, The Miracle Club,* and *The Miracle Habits.* His book *Awakened Mind* is one of the first works of New Thought translated and published in Arabic. The Chinese government has censored his work.

Twitter: @MitchHorowitz

Instagram: @MitchHorowitz23

Printed in the USA
CPSIA information can be obtained
at www.ICGtesting.com
JSHW012041140824
68134JS00033B/3190